Mary Emmerling's

Quick Decorating

Mary Emmerling's
Quick
Decorating

Text by Jill A. Kirchner
Photographs by Michael Skott
Design by Kayo Der Sarkissian

Clarkson Potter/Publishers

New York

All photographs in this book are copyright ©1997 by Michael Skott except:

Peter Vitale: 36, 37 center right, 79 top, 96 right, 99 bottom left, 118, 119 top right, 164, 168, 169 center, 169 bottom right, 192; Joshua Greene: 16, 18, 21 center right, 22 bottom right, 49 top left, 60, 67 top left, 70 top, 71 bottom, 85 top left, 100 top left, 122 bottom; Tony Giammarino: 5, 8, 32, 67 center right, 104, 107, 113 center right, 114, 125 bottom, 139, 143 center right, 160; Alan Richardson: 23 bottom right, 24 left, 26, 27 top left, 29 left, 30 top, 49 top right, 53; Jeremy Samuelson: 31 bottom, 34 right, 49 center right, 79 bottom right, 85 bottom left, 202; Antoine Bootz: 21 top left, 37 bottom right, 41, 86 top right, 116; Chris Mead: 12, 13, 15, 17; Jeff McNamara: 76, 84, 88–89; Michael Mundy: 113; Linny Morris Cunningham: 86 bottom, 93 bottom left, 131 right; George Barkentin: 11; William Stites: 2; Karen Radkai: 10

Published by Clarkson N. Potter, Inc., 201 East 50th Street, New York, New York 10022. Member of the Crown Publishing Group.

Random House, Inc. New York, Toronto, London, Sydney, Auckland

http://www.randomhouse.com/

CLARKSON N. POTTER, POTTER, and colophon are trademarks of Clarkson N. Potter, Inc.

Printed in China

Library of Congress Cataloging-in-Publication Data
Emmerling, Mary Ellisor.
[Quick decorating]
Mary Emmerling's quick decorating / by Mary Emmerling; text by Jill A. Kirchner.—1st ed.
Includes index.
1. House furnishings. 2. Interior decoration. I. Kirchner, Jill A.
TX311.E48   1997
645—dc20   96-29241

ISBN 0-517-70467-7

10 9 8 7 6 5 4

Dedicated to Carol Glasser and all the dreams of Santa Fe . . .

Acknowledgments

Everyone always asks me which of my books is my favorite—well, this is my favorite book! It is my life: I have been practicing quick decorating since I was born. I had to grow up very quickly after my father died, when I was seven. My mother worked, and I was the big sister who watched my younger brother, Terry, organized the house, ironed the clothes, cleaned, did the shopping, and had dinner ready when Mom came home from work. I loved visiting my mother at work. She ran a cotillion for the senators' and congressmen's children in Washington and worked in public relations at the Sheraton Hotel. I guess that's where I got my love for working.

Before I ever knew I wanted to decorate or even knew what a stylist was, I loved moving furniture around, changing the books and accessories in the bookcase, organizing clutter (into baskets, of course), and picking the roses in the garden behind our Georgetown house.

This book is for all my friends, roommates, lovers, husband, brother, and children, who have put up with all my moves and decorating whims.

A special thanks to:

Carol Glasser, a true friend, who helped with this book and shared her antiques with me in Santa Fe.

My brother, Terry, and my wonderful children, Samantha and Jonathan, who will soon need this book, since they are setting up their new apartments and starting their lives after college.

Juanita, who really helped move everything.

Michael Skott, who I am lucky to have known a long time and who is always a great photographer and a great friend.

Peter Vitale, photographer and friend, who has been my base in Santa Fe, and all the other photographers whose work gives life to this book— Joshua Greene, Jeff McNamara, Tony Giammarino, Chris Mead, Jeremy Samuelson, Alan Richardson, Antoine Bootz, Michael Mundy, William Stites, Linny Morris Cunningham, George Barkentin, Karen Radkai.

Jill Kirchner, for her fine writing and for understanding me so well.

Kayo Der Sarkissian, who designed the book I dreamed of.

Melissa Crowley, who has been there for lots of quick decorating!

All the dear friends and talented homeowners who opened their houses to us: Tricia Foley, Matthew Mead, Mark Clay, Lyn Hutchings, Diane Cash, Christine McCabe, Ellen Windham, Patti Kenner, Richard Goddard and Karen Bishop, Diane Brown, David Drummond, Michael Berkowitz, Donna Karan, Sandy and John Horvitz, Chris O'Connell, Jean Brooks, Carol Anthony, Beverly Jacomini, Tasha and Jack Polizzi, Susan Parrish, Mimi London, Palma Kolansky and Joe Troiano, Peri Wolfman and Charley Gold, Jimmie Cramer and Dean Johnson, Andrea Dern, Bob Smith, Duncan Brantley, Mario Montes and Jeremy Switzer, Cheryl Lewin, Sig Bergamin, Joyce Wilson, Renea Abbott of Shabby Slips in Houston, Michael Malle and Jolie Kelter, Kimberlie Waugh, Michael Foster, Orlando Roybal, Lyn Baker, Carol Ryan, Anthony Antine, T. Keller Donovan, Robert Kinnamon, and Brian Ramekers.

Gayle Benderoff and Deborah Geltman—who keep me going.

Lauren Shakely, Hilary Bass, Diane Frieden, Jane Treuhaft, Maggie Hinders, Mark McCauslin, and Joan Denman at Clarkson Potter, who do so much to make my books a reality.

And to those dreams in Santa Fe, and to Reg Jackson, who made them all come true.

Contents

Introduction

Painted cupboards, a rustic table, and a spice-drying rack "aged" a white-tile kitchen in one of our early apartments.

When I stop to think about it, much of my life has been spent honing the art of quick decorating. I got a thorough education in decorating under deadline in my many years as a home editor, author, and stylist (surely I must have a Ph.D. in it by now). On most photo shoots there is only a day, or perhaps just an hour or two, to transform a house from ordinary to camera-ready, to place bouquets of flowers into pitchers, to fill the bowls with fresh fruit, to organize clutter neatly into baskets and boxes, and to add unexpected accessories to charm the eye. "Styling" is the art of arranging these various objects into interesting vignettes that form a cohesive whole. Other books explain how to choose the paint for the wall and the fabric for the sofa; *Quick Decorating* acknowledges you may not have the time for full-scale remodeling. I will share with you the secrets of the stylist's art. These tricks of the trade may seem like small details, but they have a great impact in the way they quickly pull a room together (and draw attention away from a room's deficiencies).

But quick decorating is more than just my job; it's become a way of life. Looking back, I count at least seventeen homes I have lived in over the past twenty years—no wonder it feels like I am always moving! Some have been summer homes, some just moves around the corner, but I confess I have an itch to change my surroundings every so often. Maybe it is because my family moved often when I was a child, or maybe I just enjoy the change of scenery, and the challenge of reinventing a home. Whatever the reason, I have moved so often, and to such a variety of different places—city loft, shingled beach house, Key West cottage, Santa Fe adobe—that streamlining my decorating strategies has been a necessity. As I review my many homes, I can see an evolution in my style, but I am also surprised by how much remains constant: My quick and easy decorating principles have served me well. It all started back in the early 1970s . . .

Although I grew up amid the refined period charm of historic Georgetown, my first married apartment in New York was filled with modern furniture—chrome and glass tables, green velvet sofas. But we

soon began spending weekends in Vermont, and while my husband was off flying planes, I started scouring antique shops and flea markets. At first I bought dark, heavy oak pieces, but after I carted home a whole truckload to New York, I realized they were much too dreary and depressing for our light-filled apartment. I was able to sell it all off in one day, which taught me one of the many important benefits of buying old: Unlike new furniture, antiques don't lose their value. I then began collecting English and American country furniture instead—even back then, I sought out pieces with original paint, and humble pine tables fresh off the farm. I had a young daughter, Samantha (and would soon have a son, Jonathan), and country furnishings had a sturdy, family-friendly appeal that fit our crayons-and-cereal lifestyle. Traditional Early American wooden benches, small settees, and ladderback chairs could not accommodate my six-foot-four-inch husband comfortably, so we combined our antique finds with contemporary, clean-lined white sofas and club chairs. Our walls were also usually white, which provided a crisp contrast for peeling-paint and weathered-wood furniture. I began collecting boldly patterned handmade quilts, which I used to drape over

My daughter, Samantha, **top**, lived an American Country childhood with quilts decorating her bedroom walls.

White sofas, which became my trademark, and a log-cabin quilt lightened up rag rugs and wood furniture in our first apartment, **above**.

11

sofas, dress the beds, and hang on the walls. Expensive paintings were beyond our reach, so checkerboards, samplers, baskets, and cutting boards served as functional wall art. Rag rugs warmed our otherwise bare wooden floors, and folk art such as twig wreaths and carved wooden watermelons served as lighthearted accessories. What differentiated my approach to country, both then and now, was that I tried to keep rooms light, open, and airy, instead of cluttered, dark, and claustrophobic, as many period interiors tended to be at the time.

With the celebration of the nation's Bicentennial in 1976, and an influential Americana exhibition in New York City at the Whitney Museum that I visited many times, I decided it was important to collect furniture and artifacts from our own heritage. I turned my attention away from English antiques to focus on American country furniture. As a great-great-granddaughter of President Benjamin Harrison (who was the twenty-third president of the United States and a grandson of William Henry Harrison, the ninth president), I had never had the pleasure of living with my family's heritage; any heirlooms we had were donated to the Harrison home. I knew I wanted to collect pieces of our country's past to be able to hand down to my own children. I also made an effort to collect American folk artists whose work I felt merited greater attention.

Our home was featured in the *New York Times Magazine* in 1975 and in *House and Garden* magazine in 1978, and suddenly, everything took off. An agent, Gayle Benderoff, called to say I had a distinctive look and I should write a book about it. That phone call was the genesis of *American Country*, my first book, published in 1980, which led to fifteen more books with Clarkson Potter over the next fifteen years.

In 1981, after my husband and I divorced, I moved to a large, open loft on Union Square in Manhattan, well before it became the fashionable neighborhood it is today. There I learned that my rustic furnishings and burgeoning collections of spongeware, slipware, handwoven baskets, and wooden pantry boxes could work even in a modern space. The timeworn textures and mellowed colors of country softened the industrial edges of the loft, while its clean lines and wide-open space gave relics of the past room to breathe (a juxtaposition I revisited more

A scrubbed-pine table, large apple baskets, and place mats made from a quilt softened the industrial edge of the kitchen, **above.**

A wooden cheese rack, **opposite, above**, served as dining storage; rag rugs covered a couch, and slipware filled the shelves of the loft.

The primitive furniture and bold red-and-white scheme created the perfect backdrop for Christmas, **opposite, below**.

Tropical flowers, fresh fruit, and bar fixings suit informal island entertaining on Key West.

recently while living in the renovated Police Building in SoHo). I wrote *Collecting American Country* to help the growing number of people interested in the country look learn what it was, where to find it, and how to collect and display it—and I opened a store in Southampton, New York, to sell the treasures of the style. American country, first dismissed as another passing trend, was on a roll.

Eventually, however, one of my readers wrote to ask me, "Don't you miss your lamplight?"—meaning smaller, cozy country rooms—and I had to admit, I did. The store had expanded to a second location on Lexington Avenue, and when space opened up above it, I moved in.

CountryThen (1975)	CountryNow
Quilts	Black-and-white photographs
Slipware bowls	**Transferware platters**
Rag and braided rugs	Navajo rugs and sisal
Pewter	**Silver**
Hearts and watermelons	Crosses and tinwork
Jugs	**Urns**
Pine and oak	Painted wood and wicker
Dried flowers and wreaths	**Garden-picked sunflowers and bulbs in wooden crates**

Over time, my tastes changed, though never completely. I continued to collect American quilts and ironstone plates, and many pieces, like my blue cupboard, have stayed with me through every move. But some things naturally fell by the wayside: I stopped collecting samplers and checkerboards when I began to see them everywhere, and I finally tired of my carved watermelons. I still have my cutting boards, though they no longer hang on the wall, and baskets and boxes will never stop coming in handy for apartment living. Peg racks have hung in every house I have ever owned, and American flags are something I hope I will always treasure. The rag rugs that were a godsend with young children and pets eventually fell apart, and I began replacing them with Navajo and dhur-

My little Key West cottage was filled with light, easygoing fabrics sparked with a favorite vintage floral.

rie rugs. I was lucky to have started buying American country very early, when prices were still quite affordable. As I outgrew or accumulated extra pieces, I was able to trade up for more valuable furnishings—for example, selling off a set of firkins to buy an important cupboard.

For the past decade, my books have influenced many of my homes, and vice versa. As I crisscrossed the Rocky Mountains and Western Plains to write my next book, *American Country West*, I fell head over heels in love with the Western look rooted in our country's Native American heritage and pioneer spirit. It influenced not only my decorating style, as Beacon blankets, Western photographs, and Santa Fe crosses wove their way into my home, but also the way I dressed, as cowboy boots, turquoise and silver jewelry, and concho belts started multiplying in my closet. I came very close to buying a home in Santa Fe then, but decided it wasn't the easiest place to travel with my kids. Instead, I bought a gingerbread cottage in Key West, Florida, on a street with a name I couldn't resist: Love Lane. There, my vintage floral fabrics, painted cupboards, and pale striped sofas suited the easygoing indoor–outdoor lifestyle. Soon I was driving from Virginia to Georgia exploring the wide range of styles that comprise *American Country South*. Though Key

The heart-shaped twig headboard was a rustically romantic touch for a home on Love Lane.

Cowhide-print fabric and Beacon blanket pillows on a twig settee are a nod to the Western style I've grown to love.

My favorite benches, moved to my summer cottages, with rattan cushioned in crisp white and serapes mixed with florals.

West came to feel too far for weekending, it's kept a place in my heart.

Having a country getaway has always been an essential for me. For the past twenty-five years or so, my escape has been summering at the beach in the Hamptons on the eastern end of Long Island. I have rented and bought several houses there, including a shingled house in Bridgehampton that was brand new, but built with the same attention to detail and period features—old barn boards and beams, true divided-light windows, a large brick hearth—as houses a century ago. At the beach I mixed vintage wicker furniture with my painted wooden farm tables, and ticking stripes with romantic florals. My look has become more and more eclectic as I have incorporated new loves from every region of the country—Navajo rugs mingle with New England quilts, Southwestern ironwork with silver candlesticks, city-sophisticate leopard prints with homespun plaids—and yet it all seems to work together. The constantly evolving variety helps keep it fresh, so that I've never tired of certain things, like my painted benches or Ohio corner cupboard, that I've owned for decades.

Perhaps one of the most fun decorating challenges I have had was out-fitting a compound of four tiny cottages in the Hamptons community of

Sagaponack. While the quartet of one- and two-bedroom structures stumped most would-be buyers, I saw a wonderful opportunity to indulge each of my decorating passions, and give my teenagers (and me) our own space. Each cottage took on its own personality: Western for my son, stars and stripes for my daughter, unabashedly romantic florals for me, and neutrals for the guest cottage. The four themes were carried out through fabrics, furnishings, and accessories, but all had a cozy, cottagey feel and a breezy beachside ease. Writing *American Country Cottages* came naturally, of course.

My latest romance, and it is truly a passion I feel deep in my bones, is an adobe home in Santa Fe, New Mexico. I feel like I have truly come home when I cross the threshold of this timelessly serene, beautifully preserved hacienda. I had less than a week (four days, to be exact) to decorate this house between shoots and speaking engagements, and the fact that we pulled it off (with plenty of help from my friend Carol Glasser) is truly a testament to the power of quick decorating. I will take you on a tour of the whole process, from start to finish, in the last chapter.

In the meantime, to show you how quickly you can make a difference in your own home, I have broken down the decorating process into bite-size projects that take as little as five minutes and at most a few hours, all organized by the time required. So whether you have just fifteen minutes to spare, or a precious free afternoon, you will find decorating shortcuts and style-savvy secrets for every room in your home. Few of us have the time anymore to sew lined curtains from scratch, for example, but you can swag a drapery or tack fabric ties onto a panel in half an hour. You may not have the resources to frame and hang a wall of artwork, but you can line up a picture gallery along a shelf in short order, or pin up pictures gleaned from an art book in a matter of minutes. The time frames are meant as guidelines, not promises. Everyone works at a different pace.

This book is designed to be used in the way we all really live—with small chunks of time stolen here and there. Instead of letting a busy, pressured life leave you dissatisfied with the look of your home, you can create an inviting refuge by learning the art of decorating on the quick. The almost-instant gratification will far outlast the short time it takes to achieve.

Classic taupe-and-white sofas moved from tropical Key West to cozy Hamptons living room with ease, with the help of rich floral pillows.

A rustic cobalt bucket offers a brilliant contrast to zesty yellow lemons.

5-Minute Decorating

Even when a room has been carefully furnished, it can lack a certain ease and charm, or somehow look unfinished, or worse, uninspired. Some of the best weapons in my decorating arsenal are also the quickest and easiest to use: Pitchers of fresh flowers, bowls filled with colorful fruits and vegetables, the intimate glow of candlelight, the cozy softness of pillows and throws—these are the things I rely on in my own home, and in the many rooms I photograph, to make a house instantly look warm and welcoming. To add a colorful accent or spruce up the living room before company comes, try one of these in-a-minute miracle workers. Pillows, throws, vases, and candlesticks are also among the things I have collected religiously over the years, because they constantly come in handy. I have used my favorite paisley shawls, silver and wrought-iron candlesticks, white ironstone pitchers, and wooden mixing bowls so often and in so many different ways, I consider them members of the household. Quick decorating doesn't mean buying more; it means looking at what you already own with fresh eyes, and putting it to new use.

FreshFinds

Tomatoes, eggplants, and pears—a summer trilogy—fill a three-tiered ironstone dessert stand.

In our quest for the exotic, often expensive, decorative accessory, we tend to overlook the simple, the humble—the art in the everyday that is right before our eyes. Start with the bag of produce you bring home from the grocery store or farmstand: Instead of hiding it away in the crisper drawer, try pouring out that cache of brilliant yellow lemons or painterly Seckel pears into a bowl or a basket, or even giving them a place of honor on a pedestal or mounded into an urn. I find this approach is ideal for entertaining, since it encourages guests to help themselves—or even lend a hand in the preparation. Fresh-picked fruits and vegetables have a richness of color, a vitality and an unassuming artistry that makes them ideal for display as centerpieces, on countertops, or on coffee tables. Anywhere you would place flowers, try fruits and vegetables instead. They're inexpensive, easily accessible—and edible.

Think seasonally: A windowsill of ripening red tomatoes epitomizes summer, while a bushel of tart green apples instantly evokes fall. Consider color, shape, and texture: Line a mantel with thorny artichokes or branches of kumquats with green leaves still intact, or fill a wooden bowl with fistfuls of scarlet runner beans. Simple containers that echo the utilitarian nature of their contents are often best: Try displaying your finds on white ironstone platters or in earthenware bowls, in wooden bins and baskets from the farmstand, even in paper bags. My friend Peri Wolfman puts out an assortment of cuffed paper bags brimming with nuts and dried fruits when she entertains over the holidays, and few can resist digging in for a treat.

The more original the arrangement is, the more it will draw attention. Be bold and mix and match. Diminutive lady apples or champagne grapes can surprise in a bouquet; a few sculptural gourds or pomegranates can replace the formal centerpiece. Letting the functional take on a decorative role is at the heart of quick and easy decorating. And remember, just because it didn't take hours doesn't mean it isn't great or that you should feel guilty for having time left over to enjoy it.

Simple is as simple does: A crumpled bag, **left**, makes a humble container for fresh white beans.

Above: The beautifully variegated hues of nectarines are shown to advantage against the stippling of old shutters.

A heart-shaped woven twig basket, **left**, is just the right shape to embrace a cluster of squash blossoms.

A bushel basket of potatoes, **right**, echoes the earthy hue of terra-cotta pots on an unassuming buffet.

Sprigs of leftover holiday boxwood, **far right**, have been left to age gracefully in a cast-off wooden crate.

Peaches, apples, and candles nestled into drinking glasses creatively fill the compartments of an old wooden caddy.

A summery pairing of green limes and leaves tops off a crisp white ceramic urn.

An endearingly clever idea: This vintage wooden truck hauls a cargo of fresh asparagus stalks.

A trio of autumn
pears is nestled into
a moss-lined twig
pedestal basket,
below.

Right: Show off your
garden (or farmer's
market) bounty until
it's pressed into ser-
vice for dinner.

Styling Secrets

Abundance is essential: When you're working with something as commonplace as fruits and vegetables, seeing them in quantity is what makes a display unusual. While a single serpentine squash can be interesting, most of the time a bowlful will be more eye-catching.

Keep it fresh: Produce that needs to be refrigerated, such as asparagus, peppers, and lemons, will look fine for an afternoon until they are served, but otherwise should be kept chilled. Keep an eye on fruits and vegetables and remove any that look soft or discolored—they're called perishables for good reason!

Color is key: Whether choosing bright limes and lemons or earthier Bosc pears, let your eye be your guide at the farmstand.

Choose the right container: Seek the basket or bowl that will set off the natural beauty of the display.

FlowersUnlimited

A plentitude of pansies, from pale lemon to deep violet, are clustered in a small cast-iron urn.

It is hard to overestimate the impact of fresh flowers. To me, flowers and candlelight are what make a house a home. Flowers add beauty, romance, fragrance, an element of surprise and joy to our lives. They are a wonderful, yet affordable, luxury, and a well-placed bouquet hides a multitude of flaws in a room: It can fill dead space with color and drama, attract the eye to a focal point (and away from the dust or the drab spots), and charm even the plainest of settings.

The simplest (and quickest) bouquets are based on a single type of flower, whether picked from your garden or bought at the farmstand or florist. It might be a delicate nosegay of pansies for a bedside table, a cluster of statuesque sunflowers, or one perfect anemone in a milk bottle. Luckily, good-quality flowers are becoming more widely available, even at grocery stores. Roses are sold year-round, and are always an elegant choice. Other flowers are closely linked with the seasons: We celebrate winter's end with sunny daffodils and tiny snowdrops, and anxiously await the fragrant glory of lilacs and peonies in spring; we revel in summer's abandon with vibrant zinnias and humble daisies, and mark fall's approach in the changing hue of hydrangeas. Although I don't care for such overused flowers as carnations and mums, almost any flower used in quantity can make a dramatic statement.

Because flowers are so naturally beautiful, it is hard to make an unattractive arrangement—even if you are short of time. Simple, uncontrived bouquets are not only in fashion, but often the best way to show flowers to advantage. All you need to do is recut the stems, varying the lengths for interest, and immediately place the flowers in water. The fun comes in choosing a container. Take into account the size and scale of the flowers (hold them up against the vase or try them out before filling it with water), how many you are using, and where they'll be placed. A simple glass vase will always do, but there are also more creative options to consider. Keep a variety of pitchers and vases on hand so that you can make a quick selection when time is of the essence. When the flowers don't fit or the mood is playful, try unexpected containers: wicker bas-

Peonies, **left**, arrayed in a 1940s ceramic urn, have an overblown luxuriance that fills a room with romance.

Exquisite purple hydrangeas cluster beside a pansy-painted watering can filled with grassy stalks, **below**.

Left: Pure white tulips, in extravagant abundance, suit this clean-lined bath. Glass vases hold the blooms inside a wicker basket and beside it.

Spongeware flower-
pots tucked inside
a weathered blue
basket show
off zinnias in bold
pinks and reds.

Simple elegance: This loose arrangement of blush pink roses suits the rusticity of a timeworn chair, **above**.

A single poppy in an old milk bottle, **above right**, peers out from a cottage windowsill.

kets or wooden crates (with glass jars inside), old glass milk bottles or Coke bottles, ceramic mustard crocks, Mason jars, tins new and old, sap buckets, silver trophies, antique teapots, painted watering cans, galvanized florists' buckets, pottery mugs—almost anything that holds water will do. Experiment, and you'll develop a feel for what works best for different flowers. Blue and white spongeware shows off colorful blossoms particularly well, for example, and classics such as white ironstone, silver, simple glass, or crystal work with nearly everything. You will get perennial decorating mileage from plants, whether flowering or green, and dried flowers. I especially love orchid plants because, though pricey, they pay off in blooms that last four or five weeks.

Any room can benefit from a floral boost: A bouquet lends a welcome note of fragrance in the bathroom, where the warmth and humidity intensify its scent (and provide an ideal climate for plants). Flowers are a charming companion in the bedroom, a fresh jolt of color in the kitchen, and can bring any living room or dining table to life.

Gracefully arching orchids, delicate lilies of the valley, and tails of veronica, **above**, bring a floral painting to life.

A singular orchid creates a dramatic silhouette against the backdrop of a fan-shaped painting, **right**.

An easy route to a
dramatic arrangement,
left: Cluster several
single-variety
bouquets together.

Below: Whisper-pale
roses plucked from
the garden contrast
with bold blue-
and-white spongeware
and Chinese export
porcelain.

A poetically plain farm-
stand basket offers
up a gorgeous abun-
dance of lilac boughs,
left. Be sure to line
baskets with a water-
proof container.

Statuesque sunflowers
are a vibrant counter-
point to the spare
silhouette of a black
chair, **above**.

Two delicate garden
roses, perched in a
spongeware mug,
dwarf a diminutive
Adirondack chair, **right**.

Towering sunflower stalks, **left**, sprout from a florist's tin bucket to brighten a country porch.

Mix the ordinary and exotic: The orchid paired with blades of grass, **above**, has an Asian simplicity.

Right: Working within one color palette, zinnias and sunflowers fill an earthenware pitcher and bowl.

StylingSecrets

To anchor an arrangement: Vases with narrow necks are easier to fill and support stems best. Wide-mouth containers require a larger bunch of flowers; try a frog, florist's foam (often called Oasis, available at any florist shop) soaked in water, or a ball of crumpled chicken wire to help secure stems. You can also criss-cross florist's tape across the top of a vase to keep flowers steady (particularly if they are tall or unwieldy). Usually, however, simply interlocking the flowers' stems will be enough to hold them in place.

Begin with the outer edge: Flowers and foliage that tend to droop or bend should be placed around the edge so they cascade over the rim of the container and soften the look of the arrangement.

Embrace the dramatic: Don't shy away from tall, striking flowers and branches such as delphinium and quince. As long as you have a deep, sturdy container, these are easy to arrange and often give the greatest impact.

Time it right: If you're buying flowers for a party or special event, time their peak to your schedule. If the blossoms are full-blown when you buy them, they may look lackluster by dinner. Buy compact blooms a day or two ahead to give them time to open fully. To hasten blooming, place flowers in warm water and set them in the light. To get roses to open immediately, hold them over a steaming teapot. To prolong blooming, keep flowers in the refrigerator or a cool, dark spot.

BlanketStatements

A brilliant rainbow of stripes on a serape fans out from a stack of Mexican saltillo weavings.

Just as a shawl or a sweater can add a bit of warmth and dash to a wardrobe, a blanket or throw tossed on the sofa or draped across the bed can do the same for a room. Like pillows, throws are a softening element, and a versatile ingredient in the layered look I favor. They are a great, noncommittal way to add a jolt of color, pattern, or texture or to break up the expanse of a sofa or bed. If seating is white or light-colored, throws can help protect furniture from dog hair and paw prints, as well as people wear-and-tear. They can relieve the boredom of a practical hunter green love seat or beige ottoman without necessitating a new purchase. Larger blankets, matelassé bedspreads, quilts, or even tablecloths can be used as casual slipcovers, camouflaging a couch or chair that has seen better days. Use a throw as a "table topper," covering a solid or simply patterned tablecloth with a smaller square of fabric to add interest and depth. Throws have practical benefits, as well, as warm cover-ups for reading or napping in a drafty room.

There are wool and cotton blankets, typically smaller than bed-size blankets, specifically designed to be used as throws, but many other kinds of textiles work wonderfully as well: bold Beacon blankets, fringed paisley wraps, tapestry wall hangings, grandmothers' afghans, wool lap robes, and Navajo rugs. The newest cable-knit cotton and chenille throws feel as soft as the sweaters that inspired them. In warmer weather, light cotton throws, lacy dresser scarves, and table runners can fulfill the same functions without the weight and somber color schemes of winter woolens.

Throws and blankets can also soften the architecture of a room. A blanket draped over the stairway on a landing or displayed on the wall (using Velcro strips or a quilt hanger), or several blankets hung from a peg rack, add a note of casual warmth. Even a stack of folded blankets or patchwork quilts on top of a trunk or peeking out from a cupboard makes a room feel cozier.

Paisley throws, like Oriental rugs, seem to bring out the colors in a room and help pull them together. They work with almost anything

A richly patterned paisley throw draped across a library table, **left**, reveals its turned legs.

Sitting atop a collection of Beacon blankets, **below**, is a teddy bear cut from the same cloth.

Mix it up: A cowboy blanket and fringed damask throw, **far left**, camouflage a basket of linens.

Two plaids—on blanket and chair, **left**—surprisingly don't clash, but complement each other.

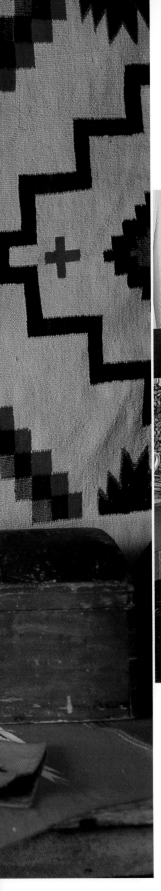

A Navajo blanket, **left**, hung on the wall makes a striking backdrop for a collection of Indian artifacts.

Tossing a Beacon blanket across the bottom of a bed adds contrast to a ticking-stripe coverlet, **below**.

because they have so many different shades woven into them. Navajo and Beacon blankets can add a hint of Southwestern spice, and their often brilliant coloring enlivens neutral or muted color schemes.

Quick decorating is about versatility; about elements that can do double—or triple—duty, without a lot of fuss. Throws are clever chameleons in that way: Today, you might wrap yourself up in an old serape as you watch a movie on television; tomorrow it might find a home hanging on the wall, covering a table, or bringing a boost of color layered atop a sisal rug.

The Navajo rug draped across an overstuffed chair, **left**, gives the white slip-cover a shot of pattern and texture.

At the ready for napping or cuddling, an old quilt softens the formality of a floral sofa, **right**.

How It's Done

A throw draped across a sofa or chair should look casual and spontaneous—a look that can be surprisingly hard to achieve. The best method I've found is to pick up the blanket by one corner, shake it out, and then throw it (or drape it) over a corner of the chair. The first time is almost always the best, so just leave it! Throws should look as if they have a sense of movement—as if they were just left there—which adds a sign of life to a room.

If you're stacking blankets, fold them in thirds so the centerpiece of the design shows. Stacked and hanging blankets should be refolded, turned over, and rotated periodically so they fade and wear evenly.

PillowTalk

A two-sided pillow-case—stars and stripes—neatly ties over a cushion to hold it in place.

Pillows are fun—perhaps because of their association with pillow fights, perhaps because they are pleasingly plump, soft and comforting, and, most important, small enough to take risks with. They can be covered in whimsical patterns, offbeat fabrics, or stronger colors than you might consider for a whole sofa. Pillows are the punctuation on play-it-safe furnishings. And while you don't want to drown a sofa or bed in an overwhelming sea of pillows, a reasonable abundance adds an aura of luxury, of plushness. Want to make your love seat look lovelier? Or your bed a little more enticing? Try piling on the pillows in a mix of prints or colors.

In the bedroom, adding a row of tall European squares with crisp shams gives a bed height and grandeur. Smaller, lace-edged boudoir pillows or neck rolls contribute a touch of feminine delicacy. And an extra set of pillows with contrasting shams, or square throw pillows in a silk damask or different texture, give a sense of bounty.

Toss pillows onto sofas and armchairs in the living and family room to bring comfort, color, or a change of pace. Oversize pillows can be used as informal seating on the floor for a group, while smaller pillows let you fine-tune the comfort level so your head is perfectly propped as you read. Dining or desk chairs that are too low or uncomfortable can be remedied with cushions (add ties to secure them in place, and use washable fabric in the dining room or kitchen). Outdoor seating can be outfitted in pillows made from weatherproof fabric such as Sunbrella. Or try terry cloth or piped canvas pillows.

Removable pillow covers (with zippers or an envelope back) offer seasonal flexibility. Cozy up with velvet, needlepoint, paisley, or leopard in winter; lighten up with cotton chintz, tea-towel plaid, mattress ticking, or lace in summer. Or use different prints on top and bottom for versatility. Pillows are instant look-changers: A basic striped sofa takes on a completely different feel depending on whether it's accented with pillows made from vintage floral bark cloth, kilim rugs, graphic batiks, or cozy quilt squares. Likewise, a vivid print chair can be toned down with solid or sedately checked cushions.

The same print in a variety of colors brightens a pile of pillows, creating a soft back for a bench, **above**.

A flag makes a great motif for a pillow. Here, Old Glory is paired with ticking stripes on a white wicker love seat, **left**.

There is a wide selection of pillows available for sale, but consider making your own for less money and more individuality. Pillows can be made from almost any kind of fabric and personalized with fringe, buttons, piping, ties, and trims.

Above all, pillows bring an inviting softness and comfort to your home. They add the kind of personal detail that makes your house different from everyone else's. And pillows are not only for people; my dog Star loves pillows almost as much as I do.

Don't be afraid to layer on pattern: Five different floral prints turn this bed into a garden, **left**.

White slipcovers are the perfect canvas for pillow artistry, **below left**. A mix of neutral patterns share a sofa.

Below: African weavings create an intricate pattern play, replacing standard back sofa cushions.

An eclectic mix of pillows—Indian blanket, American flag, seafaring chintz—proves anything goes.

Pillow ticking, once covered with a case, is now appreciated for its old-fashioned simplicity, **right**.

StylingSecrets

Don't overdo it: You don't want to have such a pile of pillows that guests have to perch on the edge of the sofa. Four to six pillows on a bed, perhaps with one or two smaller neck rolls or boudoirs, should be sufficient (a bench at the end of the bed is a good solution for storing a bedful of pillows). One or two throw pillows on a chair, and three to six on a sofa, if it is deep, give lushness without excess.

Experiment: Don't just stick with the two matching throw pillows that come with most sofas. Change their covers and add others in contrasting prints and textures. You could even consider replacing the back cushions of a sofa with an array of large square pillows for a more informal look.

The right material: The softest, most luxuriant pillows are stuffed with down, but feathers can give more body and shape to a pillow. Don't overfill pillows so that they are completely stiff, with no give, if you want them to be comfortable. Foam and Poly-Fil are the least resilient, but can be fine for small throw pillows that are mainly for show.

Keeping in shape: To fluff pillows, punch them down a few times, then karate-chop the top edge in the center, forming two peaks on either side. Or pick them up by the corners and shake up and down several times to distribute the filling evenly, then punch them in the center.

CandleGlow

A procession of wrought-iron candle-holders of varying heights lights up the length of a dining table.

This is quick decorating at its best: Nothing makes a room look more romantic and inviting with less effort than candles. Turn off the lamps, light pillars and tapers and votives, and your home takes on a magical glow. The soft light flatters faces and flatters the room, hiding bare walls, worn slipcovers, stray dust balls. Bathe every room in candlelight, from the entry to the bedroom to the bath. Line votives along a windowsill or in front of a mirror for brilliant reflection; take a pillar candle to new heights atop a column; intersperse candles among a collection on a shelf. Travel back in time with candelabra, sconces, or a candle chandelier.

On a mantel or table, instead of the standard matching pair of tapers, mass a grouping of candlesticks made from the same material—silver, crystal, wood, or wrought iron, for example. Choose candleholders of different heights and styles, or place some candles atop books or boxes, for a varied mix. To make simple tapers more special, wreathe the base with delicate greens, such as sage leaves or ivy.

An arrangement of stout, sturdy pillars of varying heights can stand alone or on pedestals. They are also ideal to intersperse among greens and fruits or flowers for a mantel- or centerpiece. To add interest to plain pillars, tie cinnamon sticks, twigs, lemon leaves, or bay leaves around the outside with raffia (keep below the level of the flame).

Votive candles can be tucked into simple glass cups (such as glass cocktail-sauce servers, available for next to nothing at restaurant supply stores), pierced tin holders that shape the light, or tiny terra-cotta pots —plain or painted gold or silver. Or, for more distinctive holders, try hollowing out artichokes, lemons, or apples. Votives are inexpensive enough to use in quantity, to dramatic effect: Line votives along the tops of deep window and door frames, up a stairway, or, for the ultimate in romance, around a bathtub or bed (carefully!).

At my house, summer nights outdoors are illuminated by starlight and candlelight, whether from citronella torches, lanterns, or votives. Old-fashioned oil lamps and hurricane shades will protect a flame in breezy weather, indoors or out. You can anchor a candle in shells,

Graceful antique sconces are a romantic source of light in an old Connecticut home.

Slim birch logs (drilled with holes), **above right**, make wonderful woodsy candlesticks.

Instant atmosphere: Tall votives, **above**, create a magical glow, illuminating a wild-flower bouquet.

Left: Candlelight from ivory tapers high-lights the sheen of sculptural wooden candlesticks and mahogany paneling.

A metal birdcage
cleverly houses
a half-dozen votives,
above, as part of an
artistic tableau.

Tall wrought-iron
pedestals with pillar
candles frame a bas-
ket of Native American
shakers, **left**.

stones, moss, or rose petals inside a hurricane, or even add shells or
petals to the oil in a glass lantern.

In summer or winter, luminaria are a charming way to line a driveway,
walkway, or edge of a terrace (though they will take a few extra minutes
to create). Luminaria can be bought ready-made or made by cutting out
simple designs in paper lunch bags. Fill each bag with a couple inches of
sand, then anchor a votive candle inside. To make ice luminaria to use in
winter, fill half a plastic milk jug with water and freeze several hours
until all but the center is frozen. Pour off any water, remove the carton,
and place a votive in the center.

I love white or ivory candles, but colors can be effective as well.
Brightly colored church candles, for example, sold in grocery stores in

An intricate Ethiopian cross flanked with silver English candlesticks creates a spare altar effect, **below**.

Small urns become holders for pillar candles, **right**, wreathed with delicate tendrils of veronica.

the Southwest for as little as a dollar, set a festive mood for summer dinners. And an ever-growing variety of interestingly striped, swirled, and hued candles expands the choices. Lightly scented candles can be soothing, especially in the bath, but never use them on the dining table, where their scent can compete with the food.

Keep a large supply of candles on hand, especially during the holidays and for entertaining. Like flowers, however, they shouldn't be saved just for company. Everyday dinners, casual cocktails, or a relaxing bath are all enhanced by the quiet, mesmerizing glow of candlelight.

Wooden balusters have been made into candlesticks, **top**, whose weathered surfaces suit sun-faded shells.

Pictures of ancestors, a golden cross, and candles create a Mexican-style altar, **above**.

A mirror and crystal candlesticks reflect the shimmering illumination of a cluster of tapers.

Candles in the bathroom, **right**, provide soft lighting and a lovely scent.

Styling Secrets

Groupings of candles often look more interesting when they're a variety of heights. To achieve the right mix, buy different-length tapers, light some a few hours ahead, use a combination of old and new, choose candlesticks of different heights, or cut off the ends of candles if necessary.

Drafts and breezes cause candles to melt unevenly and wax to spill. Don't place candles near a window, or protect the flame by using hurricane shades, votive holders, or lanterns. Bobeches or candle rings will catch ordinary drips to help protect furniture.

To unify a group of candlesticks, choose a variety of shapes all in the same material—silver, glass, wood. In general, it's best not to mix and match materials.

Instead of storing pictures away in boxes or albums, why not keep them out in a bowl for browsing?

15-Minute Decorating

At the essence of quick decorating is the possibility of change: It is liberating to realize you don't have to completely redecorate a room to give it a fresh charge of energy. Slipcovers can instantly transform the color scheme, the formality, and even the whole look of a room. Similarly, duvet covers and bed linens can reinvent the personality of a bed, taking it from the all-white serenity of summertime to a richly layered lair of paisley and velvet, and back again.

My favorite decorating ideas always incorporate the potential for change: Peg racks and propped-up picture galleries allow easy changes, whether of jackets or of art. Baskets offer the quickest, easiest way around to clean up clutter without having to buy yet another storage system or piece of furniture.

Quick decorating is not only a time-saver but a money-saver. You will probably be pleasantly surprised to find how many things you already own that can be adapted to fit new needs: Old curtains can become a duvet cover; worn-out Marseilles bedspreads can be sewn into a slipcover. And baskets and peg racks are the most economical closet you'll ever find.

Baskets, Bowls, and Boxes
ClutterControl

Stealth storage: Baskets slip beneath a table to stow blankets, magazines, newspapers.

Sometimes the secret to decorating is not just what you have out on display, but also what you put away. Clutter can ruin a room as surely as the wrong-color rug or an ungainly sofa. But finding a place for all the "extras" that accumulate—magazines, bills, correspondence, remote controls, to name just a few—can be challenging. And I like to have ready access to those things I need often (my philosophy is, if it's not out, I won't use it). For me, the solution is simple yet surprisingly successful: Find things to organize the clutter that at the same time enhance your decor. This is why I am such a fanatic about baskets—as well as bowls, boxes, and jars. These instant organizers let you clean up a space quickly and store almost anything stylishly.

Baskets have a texture and richness that typical organizing products, such as plastic bins, wire grid systems, and metal filing cabinets, lack. Baskets are a handicraft with a history; from Native Americans to the Shakers to Nantucket whalers, communities throughout the ages have put their own unique stamp on basket-making. Whether an antique bread basket, a vintage bottle carrier, or a modern-day magazine bin, baskets can be used for a multitude of purposes (see page 63). You can organize projects by basket, keeping the relevant materials pertaining to each in a separate wicker tray, for example. I even store baskets within baskets, organizing small containers of paper clips, rubber bands, thumbtacks, and other desk necessities within a larger tray. From kitchen to bathroom to bedroom, there are few places in my home that aren't filled with baskets. They allow you to tuck in extra storage unobtrusively—baskets can be stacked on shelves and bureaus, slipped on top of cupboards, stowed beneath tables and beds, lined up in closets, placed beside sofas and chairs or in corners.

Baskets work best when they are sizable and sturdy, and they look good used either in multiples of one type or in a mix of shapes and styles. There are many other types of containers that can serve similarly useful functions while looking smart: Wooden and ceramic bowls, pottery crocks, wire baskets, wooden boxes and bins, as well as glass canisters

An old utensil box serves as a portable home for silverware, making it simple to set the table outdoors.

Colorful cereal boxes are stashed in a white ceramic pail, **below**, where tiny hands can find their favorites.

Blue-and-white-check dish towels sit pretty in a spongeware bowl, **bottom**, that matches their coloring.

Left: A large, shallow basket is ideal for organizing all the magazines and books that pile up.

The charming silhou-
ettes of old-fashioned
tin cookie cutters are
on display in a clear
glass cookie jar, **left**.

Above: An old metal
pot holds summer
within: beachcombing
finds and snapshots of
favorite friends.

and jars all make attractive stowaways. Baskets and bowls also can be used to hold pinecones in winter, seashells in summer, potted plants, or potpourri. You can also use wicker trunks or stacked baskets as side tables or coffee tables (with the bonus of built-in storage). And, of course, don't forget trash baskets. If there's something I can't find, at least I know it's in a basket—somewhere.

A wire bottle carrier, **above**, makes an airy catchall in the bath for hairbrushes, tissues, and a small bouquet.

Alternative uses: A generous white iron-stone vase, **right**, holds linen napkins instead of flowers.

StylingSecrets

Here are just some of the many things you can use baskets and bowls to hold:

- Paper, pen, and address book by the phone
- Videotapes, CDs, cassette tapes
- Newspapers and magazines waiting to be recycled
- As a bar setup: for liquor and wine bottles, lemon and lime wedges, swizzle sticks
- Brushes, hair dryer, toiletries, makeup
- Toilet paper—enough so you never have to say "We're out"
- By the bed for tissues, reading glasses, maga- zines, notepad, lip balm, and lotion
- File folders—in flat trays or specially fitted baskets with hanging files
- Firewood
- Cameras and film
- Wrapping paper and ribbon
- Blankets

- Sports equipment, winter hats and mittens
- Pet needs—play toys, treats, collar and leash
- Shoes
- In the kitchen: for utensils, condiments, napkins, silverware
- Desk supplies
- Jewelry—necklaces, large bracelets
- Belts and scarves
- Work projects, expenses, tax documents, bills
- Magazine and newspaper clippings
- Stationery and thank-you notes, correspondence
- Photos—to keep out where you can browse through them, or to store those awaiting albums
- In the refrigerator, for lemons and limes, eggs, cheeses
- Cleaning supplies
- Laundry—dirty, clean, to be dry-cleaned
- In the car, for items to be taken out to the country, or back to the city

Deep baskets organize foodstuffs and cooking gear to make restaurant shelving, **bottom left**, more functional.

Round up shoes cluttering the closet floor or keep them handy by the door in a basket, **bottom center**.

Woven baskets bring texture to plain white shelves, **bottom right**, from a linen-lined one to a basket "frame."

A toolbox creates an inspired display case for natural finds such as birds' nests, **opposite**, **bottom**.

Beacon blankets are neatly stored without being hidden inside a generous-size basket.

Faded bocce balls in a wooden bin have a Shaker-like simplicity on a spare-lined bench.

Styling Secrets

Neatness counts:

While baskets tucked into shelves, atop cabinets, and beneath beds completely hide what's inside, baskets that are in view need to have more carefully organized contents. Store like items together, in neat stacks or rows, so as not to undermine the clutter-controlling purpose of the basket. This is particularly important with open wire baskets, clear glass jars, and shallow bowls and trays.

Create a lineup:

A particularly effective storage solution can be to line shelves with a row of matching baskets, such as deep wicker trays or filing baskets. The uniformity of the design enhances the sense of organization. On the other hand, when storing empty baskets—for example, above a set of cabinets —a variety of shapes, sizes, and colors makes for an interesting display.

Stay sophisticated:

Avoid ditsy, cutesy baskets that are too small to be of real use, or arrange them inside larger baskets.

RackedUp

A frieze of botanical prints underlined with a row of brass hooks is an elegant solution to entry hall storage.

Though few (if any) of us live in the simple, spare environments of the Shakers, their versatile invention—the peg rail—is just as useful in more cluttered, modern-day homes. Peg racks, a shorter version of the Shakers' rails, are the hanging equivalent of baskets: Not only do they offer a surprising amount of easily accessed storage (ideal for things like coats and towels you want to be able to grab on the go), but they also have a way of making a charming display out of whatever's hung on them. Jackets and scarves, fishing creels and canvas bags, straw bonnets and cowboy hats become a *tableau vivant* on a peg rack. I find them indispensable in an entryway, where you can also hang backpacks and gym bags, umbrellas, and cameras—anything you don't want to forget as you walk out the door. Place peg racks (or a row of hooks) beneath a shelf for extra storage, line up boots along the floor underneath, and you've got an impromptu closet. Or hang two racks, one for coats and one for hats. Keep in mind that an entrance hall or mudroom is often your first impression of a home; a peg rack can help neaten all the gear that needs to be stowed there. If you have young children, hang a lower peg rack within their reach—you'll find that children (and most adults) are much more inclined to hang a jacket up on a peg than place it on a hanger in the closet. It's the lazy person's valet.

In the kitchen, peg racks come in handy for hanging pots and pans as well as utensils and pot holders. In the bathroom, they're a welcome home for towels and robes. And in the bedroom or closet, use them to organize belts, jewelry, scarves, or exercise clothes. Hang hooks or pegs outside on the porch for beach or sports gear. Think high as well as low: Place peg racks in the unused space above doorways or cabinets, or along the edge of shelves to hold baskets or kitchen supplies.

To make more decorative use of a peg rack, prop a painting on top, tuck in a few postcards or photos, or hang a wreath from its pegs. Peg racks are ideal for drying flowers or just creating a pretty, ever-changing display of found art and favorite mementos. Think of a peg rack as a small-scale stage, where the functional gains a special kind of beauty all its own.

Skeins of vines suspended from nails, **left**, have a rusticity that suits this Early American setting.

Instant organization for an entry: A pegged shelf and roomy basket are first and last stop for jackets, boots, and hats, **above**.

Left: A Texan shelf fitted with wire hooks fills a wall with woven baskets, old tins, a fishing creel, and pack basket.

Christmas lights crown the two peg racks that form my hall "closet," filled to the brim with vibrant Western regalia.

A peg rack becomes an outdoor gallery, hung with a lighthouse painting and fishing creel and topped with a bleached cow skull.

Hooks were added to a wide wooden beam for robes in the bath, **below,** giving the utilitarian an artful air.

Bouquets of hydrangeas and roses air-dry on a peg rail, **right,** surrounded by wreaths of dried leaves.

"S" hooks run along a metal bar to keep copper pots within a cook's easy reach at the stove, **above**.

A peg rail installed along a kitchen overhang, **left,** provides an appealing perch for a collection of baskets and buckets.

Utensils hang from rawhide loops on a white wooden peg rack conveniently placed by the stove, **above**.

A long rake has been cleverly placed beneath a window to hold a gallery of assorted hats, **right**.

Styling Secrets

The right height: Hang a peg rack a bit higher than eye level, but still comfortably within reach. Peg racks that will hold primarily decorative or little-used objects can be hung even higher—beneath the ceiling or above a doorway.

Arrange carefully: As with baskets, this is organizing that's in full view. Keep items hanging neatly, and don't include things you'd rather not see every day, such as a fluorescent orange poncho. A variety of different-size items—hats and scarves with jackets—will create an inviting mix.

Keep decorative peg racks sparer: Don't overload them with tchotchkes. Allowing space around the items gives them more artistic impact.

Mix decorative with functional: Anything goes. Delicate displays like dried flowers, however, might be damaged by heavy-traffic items like coats and hats.

PictureGallery

A photograph of Georgia O'Keeffe unifies a vignette of paperwhites and a Mexican cross.

Even if a room is beautifully furnished, it doesn't feel finished if the walls are bare. The dilemma of what to hang on them can be paralyzing. Many of us are marooned in the middle ground between art posters from college and investing in "serious" art. The solution for me has often been black-and-white photographs. This affordable and accessible source of art is now also becoming highly collectible, whether the photographer is famous or unknown. Photographs work well in a wide range of settings, from modern lofts to Adirondack cabins: I have found that even in my country interiors, black-and-white or sepia-toned photographs have a crisp, graphic simplicity that provides a clean counterpoint to the rich textures and patterns of my Navajo textiles and rustic painted furniture.

You may want to focus on a theme: old sailboat pictures, or school class photos, or fences. Or you may want to collect the work of a particular artist: I own several pictures by Barbara Van Cleve, who photographs ranchers in Montana. I also treasure old portraits of Native American Indians, some of which I have simply cut from art books and framed. Or take your own photographs—buildings in your area that interest you, old or new family portraits, snow-covered landscapes—and have them enlarged on good-quality paper.

Another part of the problem is that hanging pictures is a commitment. You need to feel certain it is the right picture, in the right place, before you start pounding holes in your walls. The trend toward propping up pictures against the wall—resting them on a mantel or ledge, a bureau or table, or even the floor—makes practical as well as aesthetic sense (and, of course, it is much quicker and easier than hanging them). The casual, unstudied effect works well in today's more relaxed interiors, and it allows you a chance to "audition" pictures in a space, and interchange them at will.

These improvised picture galleries can take a variety of forms. In my last apartment, a wonderful wooden wall studded with rows of pegs became the perfect perch for my growing collection of black-and-white photographs from historical societies. I could easily add or remove pic-

An empty frame
"frames" a trio of
black-and-white
photographs, **above**.

Wooden pegs lining a
wall serve as movable
shelves for a changing
assortment of pho-
tographs, **left**.

A long hallway plays gallery to a wide range of photographs and illustrations.

Botanical prints are tacked to the wall and strung along clothes-line in an informal attic, **opposite**.

tures, or shuffle them around in order to see them anew. A friend lined the floor of his long, otherwise unremarkable hallway with a striking assortment of large black-and-white and sepia photographs and illustrations. The mix of frames, subject matter, and scale is what keeps it interesting.

A narrow ledge installed at eye level on a wall also makes a good stage for a picture display. Picture-rail molding or chalkboard railing with a wide, level upper surface works well; catalog companies such as Ballard Designs and Exposures also offer narrow picture ledges ready-made. You can also simply lean a single picture or pair of prints against a window, along a bookshelf, or on top of a bureau. It can be interesting to group empty frames with pictures or mirrors, or display them alone. Propping pictures on furniture gives them immediacy, because they are at eye level and they become a part of the tabletop tableau.

For the most impromptu solution of all, take a cue from designer Sig Bergamin, who "papered" a charming attic aerie by push-pinning pages of botanical illustrations on the awkwardly shaped walls beneath the eaves; other prints were hung with clothespins along a length of fabric tape. This would work especially well in a child's room, with a changing gallery of illustrations from favorite books or children's artwork.

SlipcoverMagic

Dining chairs that were once red-and-white check are recast in skirted linen covers that tie at the "waist."

Thanks to the slipcover craze, the idea of recovering furniture in simple, loosely fitted slipcovers is now a familiar one, but most people don't fully realize the potential slipcovers have to completely make over a piece of furniture—altering not only its color, but also its style, detailing, even shape. A tag-sale sofa with a nice silhouette but outmoded fabric can be transformed with a neatly tailored cover. Likewise, upholstered dining chairs that seem too formal for a family room can be given flirty skirts and tie-on arm covers for a breezier appeal. Leggy chairs can be skirted to the floor for a cozier look, while a tight-back sofa can let down its guard in a loose cover. A hodgepodge of mismatched chairs and sofas can be united with simple white or solid slipcovers. Formal, wintry velvets and tapestries can be "summerized" with casual canvas or striped cotton covers. Slipcovers can be as quick and easy as a large Marseilles spread or blanket draped over a sofa or chair, but they can also be as beautifully detailed as a tailored suit, with button backs, scalloped-edge skirts, or panels of mix-and-match prints. Contrasting welting, fringed trim, or self-ties can also add interesting detail. Velcro tabs and fabric ties can be added to help give loose covers a better fit.

Sewing slipcovers is by no means quick, and is not worth attempting unless you are an accomplished seamstress. Instead, I would advise scanning ads and asking friends for recommendations to find a well-priced workshop or seamstress in your area. When you consider the cost of buying new furniture, reviving an old piece with a slipcover can be a very economical choice. Slipcovers in a washable fabric are also a practical option if you have children or dogs, or have your heart set on a white sofa. Consider having two sets of covers made—for winter and summer, or solid and printed, to change the whole mood of a room. Some manufacturers now offer an additional slipcover at reasonable cost when you buy a new sofa or chair. If you like the fabrics available, it is usually a worthwhile investment. There are also one-size-fits-all ready-made slipcovers available. The elasticized models aren't especially attractive, but the unfitted panels that tie on can work well in a pinch.

A steel daybed becomes a comfortable couch, **left**, with the addition of a fitted cover and plenty of pillows.

Add charming detail: Simple chair skirts tie into place with pairs of fabric bows, **below left**.

These unfitted slip-covers, **below**, were simply made from squares of fabric tied at the back and arms.

Flirtatious skirts
that button up the
back add flair to a
set of woven dining
room chairs, **left**.

All-white slipcovers
unify disparate pieces
of furniture and make
this living room light
and bright, **above**.

Frame-back chairs
upholstered in red
velvet present a
more casual face
dressed in cotton
tie-on covers.

Similarly, a bold awning stripe on pillows and cushion dress down a gilded daybed.

How It's Done

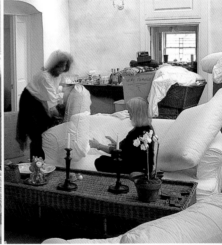

To put on slipcovers that are meant to fit snugly, it's best to slip them on after laundering while they're still a little damp so they'll stretch out firmly. If necessary, iron with spray starch. Thanks to the shabby-chic look, we're now acclimated to wrinkles—and you're going to be sitting on them soon enough anyway.

To fit pillows more easily into tight-fitting cases, fold them in half, stuff them all the way inside the cover, and then unfold them, making sure they fill out the corners.

When you're trying to get slipcovers aligned correctly on a sofa, it helps to have an extra set of hands. Make sure any piping runs straight across the sofa's lines, especially if it's in a contrasting color. You can always flip over any cushions that are stained, or camouflage them with a throw.

Begin with the Bed

Blue-and-white linens have a crisp, summery appeal; they're topped with an antique trapunto-stitched quilt.

The most prominent feature in the most personal of rooms, the bed has immediate impact. Make it look special, and the rest of the room will follow. And unlike most other furniture, its style and personality can be transformed easily and relatively inexpensively with a simple change of linens. The bed can set many moods: sheathed in crisp, all-white linens, it becomes an oasis of calm and tranquility; patterned with floral prints, it becomes a summer bower; wrapped in cozy plaid flannels and wool Beacon blankets, it evokes a rustic winter retreat.

As with a room, it is important to get the bed's bones right first. Start with a good-quality mattress, pillows, and duvet. A down-filled duvet is like topping your bed with a warm, soft cloud; it also means making the bed is a breeze (a boon for children and teens). In summer, opt for a lighter covering—a Marseilles spread, perhaps, or a handmade quilt or old-fashioned chenille bedspread. As for pillows, it is hard to have too many, as long as you have some place to put them when you want to go to sleep—a bench at the end of the bed serves well, or a nearby chair. A profusion of pillows—a backbone of tall European squares, an extra row of standard pillows, a scattering of throw pillows or boudoir pillows tucked in here and there—transforms even the most basic bed into a comforting retreat. Mix fabrics, textures, and patterns—stripes with florals, new white hemstitched linen with vintage embroidered cases, paisley prints with velvet and needlepoint. Many sheet companies now offer coordinated lines to help make pattern mixing even easier. If you prefer a simpler look, try stacking two sets of flanged or European pillows flat, side by side at the head of the bed.

Extend the same mix-and-match philosophy to sheets, duvet cover, blankets, and throws. There is no rule that says the top sheet has to match the fitted sheet, or the duvet cover. Create a more spirited pattern play by breaking up sets and blending old with new—for example, pairing a checked fitted sheet with an heirloom lace-edged flat sheet, topped with a matelassé spread or damask duvet cover. Layering is the key to a lush, inviting bed. Add on blankets or throws for soft texture:

Simplicity at its best: Pure white sheets and duvet focus attention on a weathered shutter "headboard."

This charming bed, **below**, echoes the roofline of a gingerbread cottage; textured white linens keep the look airy.

Checks and florals (note the double dust ruffle) add a hint of pattern to a lacy white bed, **above**.

A bedroom that opens onto a beautiful garden, **left**, wisely lets the flowers take center stage.

A restrained palette of khaki and white shows off the intricacy of this mahogany and wicker bed.

A lush red paisley headboard and coverlet are spiced with leopard print and vintage chenille pillows.

In a farmhouse bedroom, **opposite**, **top left**, an iron bed is dressed in ticking stripes and a bevy of pillows.

The unusual placement of this bed lets light stream in through its iron railings, **opposite, top right**.

ethereal mohair, thick cable-knit wool, or velvety chenille. A duvet or quilt can be folded or layered over a bedspread; blankets can be draped or stacked at the bottom of the bed. The trick is to show the layers to advantage, not hide them beneath a long, boring expanse of comforter. Fold the top sheet down over the top of the duvet, rather than tucking it in, creating a deep border, or fold the duvet halfway down the bed to reveal more of the blankets and linens beneath. The most inviting beds are not the perfectly made ones that you could bounce a quarter on, but the more casual ones, with rumpled covers and cozy blankets, personalized with small pillows, sachets, or even a stuffed teddy bear.

StylingSecrets

The finished look:

Don't overlook the importance of a dust ruffle for polish and to create a hiding place for underbed storage. It can be anything from a tailored, box-pleated bedskirt to a flounced and ruffled pettiskirt. Don't feel limited by the few ready-made options. You can fashion a bedskirt from sheets, coverlets, vintage table linens, lace, or almost any fabric. Sew one up using a fitted sheet as the base, or just fake it by tucking in fabric between the mattress and box spring. Try layering two skirts of different lengths (a full-size skirt atop a queen-size, for example) for a more lavish effect.

Try an alternative: If

you prefer a simpler look or your bed frame doesn't accommodate a dust ruffle, place a second fitted sheet, in a matching or contrasting color, over the box spring for a tailored touch.

Shifting with the sea-

sons: Change the look, and layering, of your bed with the season. All-white linens with a simple piqué bedspread are the epitome of summer, but you could just as easily choose soothing sherbet hues, bright cabana stripes, or romantic florals. In winter, flannel sheets in woodsy plaids are a cozy choice, while rich paisleys, leopard prints, and jewel-toned jacquards are more sophisticated warm-ups. Build a wardrobe of linens with an eye to mix-and-matching by buying an assortment of extra flat sheets and pillow shams (new or vintage) instead of sets of sheets. It will save money and inspire variety.

The draped bed:

Dress the bed in curtains or canopies for a more romantic or intimate feeling. If your bed has no posts or canopy, drape fabric from curtain rods or the wall above the headboard, or hang mosquito netting (it often comes affixed to a ring you hang from the ceiling). On a four-poster bed, instead of traditional frilly canopies, try hanging or draping simple, straight panels of plain muslin or cheesecloth for more understated elegance.

All-American red, white, and blue linens and a mattress-ticking cover take their cue from the flag.

Instead of a Bed

While there are a wide range of beautiful ready-made beds, from mahogany sleigh beds to wrought-iron confections, you can also give a bed character and imagination (for less expense) by creating your own headboard for a basic bed frame.

Investigate the salvage yard: Wonderful headboards can be fashioned from old arched shutters, a wrought-iron gate, a section of picket fencing, carved boiserie panels, Palladian window frames, or wooden garden trellises.

Enlist a work of art: Hang a large painting, mirror, quilt, or a flag on the wall above the bed to create the dramatic effect of a headboard.

Secure your investment: A headboard should be carefully anchored to the wall or bed. Lightweight headboards can be nailed or screwed into the wall; very heavy ones, such as an iron gate, should be bolted into the studs. Hire a carpenter or handyman if you are in doubt about how to do it.

The art of arranging interesting tableaux transforms a simple glass table into a visual feast.

30-Minute Decorating

Decorating is often assumed to be a task of gargantuan proportions—a process that requires unlimited time, money, and patience. And taken all at once, it is overwhelming. But decorating is both easier and more enjoyable when approached as a series of small endeavors. You can gain much more satisfaction from dressing your windows, rearranging your fireplace mantel, or hanging prints in half an hour than you could shopping for elaborate furnishings for a week—and instead of sapping your enthusiasm, the sense of accomplishment will give you energy to take on the next mini-project. This chapter provides answers to many of the decorating questions I'm most frequently asked, such as how to dress windows simply but stylishly, how to camouflage impossible-to-store items like exercise bikes, and the age-old hunt for a coffee table that is functional yet not typical.

Decorating is in the details, and the process of styling and arranging objects can be broken down into simple steps that anyone can accomplish with a little practice. The art of arranging is one that comes in handy in a multitude of places, from creating a charming coffee-table tableau to fashioning a striking centerpiece. It also offers the satisfaction of feeling that you have created something special from almost nothing.

Vignettes
The Art of Arranging

Beside the bed, photos are unexpectedly tucked into a pitcher and placed atop books; tissues nestle in an old tin.

One of the things I am best known for as a decorator and stylist is creating interesting displays of objects on anything from coffee tables to bureaus to a bathroom vanity. These finishing touches make the difference between a standard room and a special one—and they don't have to take a lot of time. You can usually work with what you already own to create an inviting arrangement. While it is often assumed the art of composition is a talent you are either born with or not, I believe there are some simple guidelines that can help anyone fashion creative tablescapes. The other secrets to success are practice, and developing a good eye. When you see an arrangement that appeals to you, whether a store display or a tabletop tableau in a shelter magazine, take a moment to study it carefully: Take note of how elements are grouped together, how various materials and textures are juxtaposed, and how different sizes and scales are interwoven. Instead of just flanking a painting with a couple of candlesticks, a few more minutes' work can make all the difference. Try elevating the candlestick on a stack of antique books, propping a small framed picture against them, and adding a vase of delicate flowers. The more you experiment and improvise, the more interesting compositions you will eventually create. It doesn't require expensive collectibles or valuable family heirlooms; many times the most interesting elements are all around us—river-smoothed stones, shells from the beach, a bowl of fresh apricots or dried rose petals. In photographing a multitude of variously equipped houses, I've learned to be resourceful: Fill a big wooden salad bowl with bundles of twigs, or an old watering can with leafy branches. Stack up books instead of shelving them, and remove the jackets to reveal their bindings. Drape a large scarf across a table or a necklace atop an open book. I'm not advocating clutter or overstuffing a house with meaningless "things"; in fact, I think empty space and bare surfaces are essential to appreciating objects of importance. But with careful arrangement, those objects can have a unified, aesthetically pleasing presence instead of looking like a mishmash of unrelated knickknacks.

Paintings of flowers in frames and on watering cans are interspersed among the real thing, **top.**

Left: A silver pitcher brimming with roses contrasts with a peeling table and a mix of frames.

Rustic color unites a worn chest and birdhouse with sunflowers and apples, **above.**

Top: Each column of books on a table is topped with a different object, centered by a candelabrum.

Making the most of an ottoman, **above,** books are layered with a tray, bowl, magnifying glass, and more.

Seaside charm characterizes a candlelit arrangement with a shell-covered box, frame, and vase.

StylingSecrets

Here are steps for taking the everyday objects around you and creating a still life to inspire any artist.

Start with the existing elements:
In any room, furniture and objects are naturally needed in a particular spot. On a bedside table, for example, might be a lamp, a clock, a small porcelain dish for safety pins and coins, a basket for tissues and lotion, pictures of family and friends. On a dresser, the basics might be a mirror and a jewelry chest or baskets for baubles, a silver tray with toiletries.

Group like items:
Instead of scattering your children's silver baby cups or small boxes collected on trips, bring them together in one place where they can have a greater impact, and use them as the core of a display. To give focus to a disparate assemblage—for instance, on a bureau— organize small items inside larger containers, such as a tray or shallow basket. Find special containers for mundane necessities, like a hand-blown glass or ceramic mustard crock for cotton balls and swabs.

Create a focus:
If a collection is not the core of your composition, choose a particularly bold or striking item that will be. It might be the largest item, such as a statuesque vase or candlestick, or the one with the most intriguing form, like a carved bust or large starfish. It should not necessarily be placed dead center; asymmetrical arrangements are often more dynamic. And as you build your grouping, this piece will be balanced by other elements.

Layer textures:
Add in other items that create textural contrast, such as worn leather picture frames, a tortoiseshell box, woven wicker baskets, wooden candlesticks. The soft folds of a velvet tablecloth, the glow of votive candles, the scent from a small bouquet or dish of potpourri can all add to the sensory richness.

Add height:
The often overlooked key to an interesting composition is to use items of different size and scale. Layer items vertically to give them variation in height. A stack of books

A sailboat model
is the centerpiece of a
naturalistic tableau
with a horn candle-
stick and leafy lamp-
shade, **below.**

Right: Native Amer-
ican handicrafts are
invitingly arrayed
around the perimeter
of a primitive table.

makes an excellent pedestal for candlesticks, small ceramic vases, or a picture frame. Place a plant atop a wicker basket, or make a vase stand taller by stacking it on an overturned bowl. Give a small statue or a silver urn a lift by placing it on a wooden chest. This also solves storage problems in a small space by letting you house more things on the same piece of real estate.

Emphasize form:

Leave breathing room in which to appreciate the silhouette of an architectural fragment, a sculptural wire topiary base, or an outstretched orchid. Your arrangement should not be so dense that it obscures the shape of individual components.

Bring it to life: Whenever

possible, add elements from nature—cut flowers or a small topiary, seasonal fruits or vegetables, even autumn leaves gathered on an afternoon walk—to give an arrangement freshness and immediacy, as well as a connection to the world outside. Fragrant flowers and herbs enhance its sensory pleasures as well.

Top it off: I rarely leave a

flat surface alone. Atop a stack of books I might place a cross from Santa Fe, a horn-handled magnifying glass, or a pair of match strikers. Weight the pages of an open book or create the final flourish on a stack of boxes with a shallow bowl; a small picture frame, laid flat; a diminutive cherub; a fossil or conch shell; or some other treasured talisman from a journey.

The ultimate goal: to

create a balanced, harmonious composition in which the different items complement each other rather than compete. If one item seems out of scale with the others, or inappropriate for the setting, or if the arrangement is becoming too cluttered, remove whatever doesn't work. It is easier to create a compelling tableau with a few interesting items than a dozen mediocre ones. And keep changing things around; a stiff, formal composition lacks the energy of an impromptu one.

Vignettes
Arranging Collections

Silver perfume bottles
and dresser jars
fill every inch of a tiny
table with charm.

Collections reflect our private passions, our quirks of preference or personality, our personal history, or our aspirations, embodied in tangible objects. You may not even realize you have been collecting, until suddenly one day you notice that your cupboard holds a dozen pitchers, or trade blankets, or trinket boxes. My favorite collections are of functional items like tolework trays, wire baskets, silver candlesticks, or spongeware bowls that can be put to use while looking pretty. Items with a practical side may be assigned to useful spots throughout the house, but in general, collections benefit from being displayed together in one place.

When considering where to display a collection, look beyond the obvious bookshelves and cupboards (though they, too, are effective choices) to find an inspired setting. Plates and trays can be hung on dining room or kitchen walls, gracing the room until they are needed on the table. Unusual collections—old toys, cookie tins, or signs, for example—might bring a shot of color or creativity to a den, home office, child's room, or even a powder room. Seek out unexpected spots above kitchen cabinets or doorways, lining the stairs or a porch railing, framing a doorway, or covering a hallway. If you have a large collection or one of small or unusually shaped objects, old store display cases, library card catalogs, apothecary cabinets, and other commercial fixtures can provide a distinctive venue. Certain collections, such as old textiles, may have special storage considerations—and can look just as intriguing lining the shelves of a cupboard. Quilts or blankets could be hung over a railing or ladder; teapots or miniature chairs might perch on small ledges across a wall; baskets or pots could be hung from hooks along ceiling beams; glassware sparkles when placed near a window where it can catch the light. Arrange items to show each to advantage, while keeping it part of the whole. Overstuffed cupboards can smother a collection, while an airy lineup leaves room to savor each object's silhouette. Collections are often best appreciated if you rotate items, keeping some in storage and some on display, or occasionally changing their locations or arrangement, so you see the pieces anew.

Narrow shelves are just the right size to display a lineup of antique bottles.

Old trellis frames become graphic wall art hung in an intersecting arrangement, **below.**

Beaded Indian pouches in a similar color palette are casually grouped with natural artifacts.

Hand-carved canoe paddles and other woodsmen's relics reside on the walls of a rustic cabin, **above.**

This armoire's open-
door policy shows off
a collection of Indian
and Beacon blankets
while protecting
them from sun, **right.**

Stairs become a show-
case for a step-by-
step assembly of bird-
houses, **far right.**

Indian weavings
are displayed from
floor to ceiling, used
as rugs, throws,
and wall hangings.

An old set of mailboxes creates the perfect cubbyholes for vintage fishing buoys and floats.

Far left: American flags of varying ages are tucked into baskets to brighten a corner with patriotic cheer.

Please be seated: Two benches appropriately host rows of miniature chairs, making clever use of a landing, **left.**

Functional collections of yelloware bowls and a variety of platters create warmth in a kitchen, **opposite, above.**

A glass ledge running across a window, **opposite, below,** becomes a perch for majolica vegetable pitchers.

The vivid greens and yellows of this majolica collection, **below,** brighten the shelves of an antique hutch.

MirrorImages

An intricately carved and gilded mirror reflects a beautiful dining vignette.

Mirrors are the magicians of decorating: They can make a space look larger and lighter; they double the impact of any element they reflect, whether fresh flowers or a beautiful view; they can fill an unremarkable space with refinement and drama. Although practical considerations may dictate size and shape, what gives a mirror style is its frame. It may be anything from simple molding with rustically peeling paint to elaborately carved and gilded filigree. Because it can be difficult (and costly) to find old mirrors—especially large ones—in good condition, I have found it is often easier to use a picture frame, whether found at a flea market or a framing shop, and have it fitted with a mirror, which many framers and glaziers are equipped to do. In addition to picture frames, architectural elements, such as interesting windows, can also be fitted with mirrors instead of glass.

Mirrors are a classic choice above a sofa or mantel, and hanging a large mirror on a wall adjoining a window will help reflect light into the room. Mirrors are particularly welcome in small, dark, or awkwardly shaped spaces such as halls, entries, and bathrooms, where they can help maximize light. Mirroring a wall is a good way to expand the sense of space in tight quarters, but don't overdo it: You don't want to feel like you're in a 1970s discothèque. If you have a mirrored wall that seems too cold, consider hanging an empty frame on top of it for a whimsical note. (You can affix lightweight frames using Velcro strips; for heavier frames, have a glass cutter install screws for hanging.)

The bathroom is a natural home for mirrors. Instead of a utilitarian medicine chest, consider hanging an elegant gilded mirror, and install shelves or a cabinet for storage. The wall above the bathtub (if it is not a shower wall) is often charmed by the addition of a generously sized mirror. If the bathroom door has raised panels, they can be fitted with mirrors to unobtrusively brighten the space. (This works well on a closet or inside a bedroom door, too.) In bedrooms, a full-length mirror is usually a must, whether it is a freestanding cheval glass or a mirrored door. Place smaller mirrors above a bureau or on a dressing table to provide a close-up view.

Prop up an oversize
mirror on the floor
for unstudied drama,
above.

Old mirrors in good
condition are rare
finds, so consider hav-
ing an antique frame
fitted with a new mirror
instead, **left.**

A fragment of an elegantly arched window is fitted with mirrored glass, **left,** in designer Donna Karan's house.

Flowers placed beside a mirror appear twice as nice, **above**.

An ornate empty frame calls attention to a clean-lined antique mirror, **right.**

An array of intricately framed small mirrors, **far right,** is an appealing alternative to the standard mirror above a bureau.

Intriguing architectural salvage finds such as a carved medallion make one-of-a-kind mirror frames.

A Gothic window
frame gives shape to a
mirror that reflects the
well-worn surfaces
around it, **above.**

Two mirrors, one oval,
one square, surprise
when placed one in
front of the other, **left.**

In an airy white room, **below,** a wall of mirrors helps further increase the feeling of light and openness.

A tall, narrow mirror, **right,** is an elegant way to fill the empty space between sets of French doors or windows.

Styling Secrets

Think big: For greater impact, particularly in a living or dining room, prop an oversize rectangular mirror on the floor, adjacent to a sofa or chair.

When small is better: In a limited space, for example, between two doors in a hallway, or above a bedroom dresser, hang a collection of small mirrors or hand mirrors on a wall.

Switching shapes: Don't get stuck in a rectangle rut; round and oval mirrors can be a softer, surprising choice.

Perfect reflections: Consider what will be reflected in the mirror before hanging it. You won't want to see cluttered shelves or the recycling bin. By contrast, it is always a nice idea to place flowers or candles in front of a mirror, where they'll seem twice as lush and inviting.

WindowDressing

An embroidered panel made from a vintage sheet is gathered onto a swing rod for a simple, movable window treatment.

What windows should wear is an all-too-familiar decorating dilemma, especially if you want something softer and more stylish than the ubiquitous metal mini-blinds but you can't abide frilly swags and pleated drapes. To my mind, the best window treatments are often the most basic: Simple panels let in light, rather than obscuring it, and don't upstage a beautiful view. Inexpensive fabrics, such as muslin, unlined linen, sheer gauze, or sturdy canvas, can be fashioned into plain, unpleated panels. Hang them with wooden or iron rings or fabric tabs on a wooden or wrought-iron pole. For the quickest curtains of all, use clip-on curtain rings or just sew a casing at the top of the fabric panel. I made muslin curtains with an additional casing sewn partway down the panel so that the curtain can be hung at two different heights; the extra material folds over into a soft cuff of fabric at the top.

The simplest window treatments don't even require a sewing machine. A generous length of fabric can be swagged across two large hooks or brackets, and left to drape luxuriously down each side of the window. Old lace tablecloths, linen bed sheets, dresser scarves, or vintage curtains may be close enough in size to use on your windows without alteration; and ready-made curtains are becoming available in simpler, tailored styles at affordable prices.

To add a fillip of interest to plain or ready-made curtain panels, sew trim or old lace to the edges, stitch on a border or lining of contrasting fabric, or use interesting tiebacks fashioned from fabric or braid, or metal holdbacks.

If greater privacy is required, consider using louvered shutters, neat Roman shades made up in a neutral fabric, or old-fashioned wooden blinds. You can also fashion fabric shutters on swing-arm rods for an elegantly simple look. These are a good option for French doors and casement windows, where traditional curtains or shades can get in the way.

Beyond curtains, glass shelves lined with bottles, a panel of stained glass, a profusion of ivy vines, or a small folding screen can effectively provide privacy at a window while adding an element of interest.

A cheerily striped
bed curtain also
serves as an informal
room divider in this
one-room cottage, **left.**

Bottles lined along
windowsills, **below,**
capture the glow
of lamplight at night.

Country simplicity:
Cotton tab curtains
hung on a wooden
rod suit the all-white
informality of this
home, **left.**

Gauzy curtains edged in seashells hang from the ceiling to create a private oasis in an attic bedroom, **left.**

Sheer panels simply tacked in place bring wispy romance to a set of undistinguished windows, **below.**

A Roman shade forms
a neat valance when
raised, well-suited
to the crisp stripes in
this bedroom.

A canvas panel becomes a versatile shade with a set of grommets and hooks.

HowIt'sDone

For an easy, utilitarian, yet fresh approach to window treatments that is perfect for a beach house or other casual setting, hang plain canvas panels onto a series of hooks. Attach grommets, buttonholes, or fabric loops along the top of the fabric panel, and then affix corresponding cup hooks or wooden pegs to the window frame. Hang the curtain panel on one, two, or more hooks depending on how much privacy and light you desire. If you run a row of grommets or buttonholes along the bottom of the panel as well, you can "raise" the shade by looping the bottom grommets on the hooks. All kinds of variations are possible: one corner peeking up, both corners joined in the center (see top photo), or all three grommets evenly hooked to the top. Grommets and grommet pliers are available at sewing stores.

WorksofArt

A shuttered cabinet frames a landscape painting, creating the transcendent effect of a window.

When a display of art more permanent than propped-up photographs is required, hanging pictures is still the tried-and-true method. Hanging pictures will allow you to cover a larger area, to create an arrangement that stretches both vertically and horizontally, and to give the picture itself more permanence or formality.

I generally prefer simple frames—black or natural woods such as cherry, walnut, or pine, or an occasional gilded frame. But frames can be works of art in and of themselves. You can often find beautiful old frames at tag sales and flea markets. If they are well priced, they may be worth buying just for the frames, even if you don't like the pictures inside. I have also found many paintings I love (I collect flower paintings, in par-ticular) whose frames I didn't care for. Removing the pictures and hang-ing them as unframed canvases gives them an unstudied charm.

Choosing frames is largely a matter of personal preference, and a good framer can help you determine what's right on a picture-by-picture basis. But don't select a frame without considering the context—where it will be hanging. Take photographs of your room to the framer, so she can get a sense of your decorating style. Don't frame pictures in sleek black metal frames if your room is filled with delicate floral prints; gold or natural wood would be more appropriate.

Photographs framed with a fairly wide mat—at least two or three inches, depending on the size of the picture—look more artistic to me than narrow (or no) mats. Pictures can also be double- or triple-matted for greater emphasis and depth. And framing doesn't have to be expen-sive. There are many good ready-made frames available in a range of sizes. A great money-saver is to buy a ready-made frame but have the mat custom-cut, to give pictures a more professional appearance.

When you are ready to hang your pictures, start by laying them out on the floor to devise an interesting arrangement. Picture-hanging is often most successful when done in relationship to a piece of furniture or an architectural element in the room—in the tried-and-true spots above the sofa or mantel, for example, but also between a pair of windows,

Traditional paintings have a fresh appeal hung from bookcases rather than walls.

A series of black-and-white photos of architectural details is hung in an appropriately geometric grid, **below.**

A trio of old sepia pictures, framed in richly grained wood, **above,** is crowned by a pair of steer horns.

Vintage photographs of sports teams, **left,** make an entertaining display on the wall of a bath.

next to an armchair in the corner, or running above a set of bookshelves or the wainscoting. Pictures can also be chosen to fill an empty space, perhaps at the top of the stairs, or to fill an entire wall, in a hallway or library. Related works can be hung in a pair or series of three or more. Even the most inconsequential pictures can gain impact grouped in a large series, in a grid of nine or even a dozen.

It helps to imagine an invisible axis, or axes, running vertically or horizontally through your arrangement. Work up from a baseline such as a chair rail or piece of furniture; down from a picture rail or molding; or out from the center of a cross-shaped axis. Play around with possibilities until you're happy with an arrangement, then map out where it will be hung on the wall. I think pictures are often positioned too high: I like to view artwork at eye level, and if a particular painting will generally be seen from a seated position—a sofa or dining table—then it can go even lower.

Once you've determined the spot (draft an extra pair of hands and eyes to help you judge), put a light pencil mark on the wall at the top of the frame. Then measure from the top of the frame to the picture hanger or picture wire (fully outstretched, as it will be when it hangs) and mark that point below your first mark on the wall. This is where to hammer in your picture hook. The most stable method (especially for large pieces) is to hang a picture with two nails or hooks, to avoid having to straighten it constantly.

Black-and-white photographs and engravings are hung in an artistically random yet connected fashion, **far left**.

Floral paintings, framed and unframed, are loosely grouped around a wicker table of flower-rimmed mirrors, **left**.

StylingSecrets

"Art" isn't just what hangs in museums. Here are some sources for photographs and prints to fit any pocketbook:

Research the past:

Many local historical societies have photographic archives that sell inexpensive 8-by-10-inch reproductions. The Library of Congress and the Historical Society of Washington, D.C., also have vast libraries of photographs available to order.

Hit the books:

Art monographs and coffee-table books are often a treasure trove of pictures, whether photographs, illustrations, or engravings. For forty dollars (or considerably less, if it's secondhand or paperback) you might get twenty pictures worth framing. Share with a friend or give them as gifts. Similarly, well-produced calendars, such as the oversize ones printed by Archiva, offer a dozen ready-to-frame images.

Displays:

Department stores often sell off the props in their model rooms at the end of the season; that's how I snagged the two museum-quality photographs of Native American chiefs over my sofa.

Art fairs and student shows:

Art schools, in particular, often have end-of-year exhibitions showcasing up-and-coming talents —at affordable prices.

Tag sales and flea markets:

Another source for artwork and other frameables are outdoor sales. Look for old maps, magazines, menus, charts, ledgers, and advertising cards. Some of today's most collectible art—architectural renderings, botanical drawings, fashion illustrations, furniture designs, and catalog art—were once considered castoffs.

Quick Fixes
Create a Coffee Table

The legs of an old English pine table were cut down to create a commodious coffee table, **above.**

A tavern table, **right,** was cut down just a bit to form a coffee table that's still high enough for casual dining.

The quest for an attractive coffee table often seems to be a daunting one. Perhaps because coffee tables are a relatively recent invention—you can't just dig up a nineteenth-century antique—it's hard to find something with a little more character than the standard wood or glass-topped rectangular tables. The coffee table has taken on increasingly more importance in living and family rooms, often doubling as an informal dining table, storage for books and magazines, footrest, and display case. One way to avoid decorating clichés is to cut down an old wooden kitchen or small dining table to coffee-table height (about 19 inches, even higher if you like to dine there). This provides a generous-size table with more warmth and personality than a new ready-made table. I sometimes use old benches for the same sense of character. Other possibilities: a wrought-iron garden table; an oversize ottoman; a wicker or wooden blanket chest; a piece of glass or wood perched atop iron garden urns or a pair of pedestals; two or three small occasional or nesting tables instead of one large coffee table; a steamer trunk or stack of old suitcases. I have even used the base of a wicker chaise longue for a coffee table. Keep your eyes open for other less expected possibilities, whether a pair of handcrafted stools or a large Pueblo drum.

A low drop-leaf table, **left,** can scoot up to the wall when space is at a premium.

Large garden urns make a distinctive base for a glass-topped table, **below.**

Rustic benches stacked atop each other, **left,** can serve as impromptu tables or shelves.

Quick Fixes
ScreenSavers

A folding screen made from wood panels covered in damask fabric closes off an alcove kitchen.

Need to camouflage a corner filled with file boxes or an exercise bike? Want to add another dimension to a boxy room? Looking to section off space for an office or dining area? The folding screen—an old-fashioned decorating device that is coming back into favor—may do the trick. Screens can inject height, angles, and drama into a plain-Jane space, serve as a portable and inexpensive room divider, conceal clutter or an unattractive view, or create an interesting backdrop where there was once a dead corner. Screens can be found ready-made, or they can be easily constructed using old shutters, doors, wooden panels, stretcher frames covered in fabric, or Shoji screens. Attach hinges between each set of panels so that they open in alternating directions, creating an accordion effect. Plain panels could be covered in fabric (staple-gun along each edge, then glue trim along exposed edges) or wallpaper; a scenic mural could be particularly striking. Or create a memory-board screen by crisscrossing lengths of ribbon across each panel; tack in place with upholstery tacks (see "Outfitting a Home Office"). You could also hang a column of framed photographs or prints joined, by a length of ribbon, on each panel, or decoupage prints or book pages directly onto a wooden screen. Panels with an interesting profile can lend a more architectural quality, but sometimes just the texture of worn paint on old shutters or doors is all the interest that is needed.

A painted botanical screen (which could also be made with wallpaper), **right,** conceals the toilet in a bathroom.

This screen has been crisscrossed with ribbon, **left,** to create a bulletin-board backdrop for a desk.

An oak screen paneled in shirred muslin, **below,** lets in soft light, but conceals the television.

Quick Fixes
LightIdeas

A dressmaker's mannequin has been adapted into a fashionable floor lamp.

There are more options for interesting lighting than ever before, running the style gamut from rustic to high-tech, but a more personalized possibility is to have a lamp made from a piece of your choosing. Lamps can be created from almost any sturdy base: a salvaged baluster, cast-iron urn, wire topiary form, alabaster vase, large wooden candlestick, art pottery or earthenware crock, china teapot, country birdhouse, or watering can. If you're a do-it-yourselfer, there are lamp-making kits available at lighting-supply and crafts stores, but if the item is valuable, or it isn't hollow, you're better off having it done at a custom-lamp shop.

You can also personalize a store-bought lamp easily and inexpensively by customizing the shade. Again, there is an increasing variety of charming ready-made shades available, but it's an easy project to do yourself. I've seen shades adorned with old photographs or slides, covered in wallpaper or fabric, trimmed with rawhide stitching or fringe, hand-cut in stenciled patterns, papered in old maps or blueprints, decorated with decoupaged or rubber-stamped motifs, even covered in artificial rosebuds. Using a standard lampshade as your base, look for a simple, not overstated, motif that will work with the room. Place the shade on the lamp, lit, to work, so you can see how it will look illuminated. Using spray adhesive (for papers and fabrics) or a glue gun (for trims and heavier elements), affix the decorative elements to the shade. Sometimes just changing the color or size of a lampshade—from white to black, or to a smaller, more tapered shape—can make all the difference.

Black lampshades often look more striking than white; the candlestick base is a classic, **right.**

The mannequin lamp
is dressed to shine,
left, in a fringed jacket
and strands of beads.

Adorned with old fam-
ily photographs and
cameras, a lamp
becomes a home for
memories, **above.**

Bookshelves sprinkled liberally with family photographs and travel souvenirs invite the eye closer.

1 Hour to an Afternoon

Certainly there are times when renovation or top-to-bottom redecorating is in order. But much of the time, when a room is essentially sound, or the home is a rental, or budget constraints have reared their ugly head, small decorating changes can have a surprising amount of impact. If you hate your kitchen cabinets or your bath hasn't been updated since the 1940s, there are still ways to fill those spaces with warmth and charm. Similarly, if you dream about adding on a home office or hiring someone to come in and organize your closets, think again: You may be overlooking an existing corner in which to house a desk and files, or underestimating what you can accomplish in your closets on your own.

Tackling larger problems is much like solving the smaller ones—it is often still a matter of using simple styling touches to make a countertop, then cabinets, and, eventually, the whole room look better. With just a little more time to devote to the task, you can take on bigger decorating projects and problems, such as kitchens and baths, still using a quick-and-easy approach to solving them.

Bookshelves
LinedwithCharm

Native American artifacts bring the topics of a book collection to life, and create a caesura of space.

Rows of shelves filled top-to-bottom with books are well-suited to libraries, but in a living room or bedroom, bookcases should be a decorative element in their own right. The difference between creating mundane shelfscapes and inviting ones is often a simple matter of leaving space around books, instead of stacking them end to end, and interweaving intriguing objects that add texture and surprise. Not only do shelves serve as a worthy storehouse for items too pretty to be hidden away in a closet, but these objects—picture frames, baskets and boxes, candlesticks, plates, folk art pieces, plants—create a more varied and eye-catching terrain within the rectangular regularity of boxlike shelves.

Arranging bookshelves is similar to arranging vignettes, but is done on a broader canvas. I like to marry objects of wide-ranging variety, but with a general underlying theme in mind. In my new home in Santa Fe, which is filled with bookshelves, a prominent wall of shelves in the hallway became a stage for my collection of blue-and-white transferware platters and spongeware pieces, as well as books, baskets, and bowls. The blue-and-white color scheme stands out beautifully against the white painted shelves, lightening and enlivening stacks of books that, on their own, could be oppressive in such a small space.

Cabinets and cupboards, whether filled with china, collections, or necessities, can be organized in much the same way: Remember to leave some open space on shelves, and to meld a variety of textures— shimmering silver, earthy ceramics, woven wicker—and surfaces both dark and light, patterned and solid, to intrigue the eye and avoid a sense of sameness or repetition.

The tops of bookshelves, cupboards, and cabinets can also serve as surprisingly functional storage and display space. A row of oversize bowls or an assemblage of baskets can help fill that awkward space between cabinet tops and the ceiling with artful flair, while providing space for large items otherwise not easily accommodated. These sorts of high-reach galleries can help stretch the horizons of a small room upward, or fill the bare, chilly reaches of a large room with warmth and detail.

A window is framed by book-lined shelves, **left,** with a few eyecatching objects placed on top.

Primitive painted shelves, **above,** are stacked with books as well as colorfully graphic quilts.

A cracked and peeling Western cupboard, **left,** is home to an informal arrangement of woodsy majolica.

Built-in shelves create
a cozy niche for
a sofa, with an upper
"valance" lined with
picture frames, **left.**

A huge Irish dresser
brimming with
Staffordshire china,
above, becomes the
focal point of a room.

Screen doors on
a Mexican cupboard,
right, reveal rows
of exuberantly colored
Beacon blankets.

Everything needed
to set the table
is artfully—and hand-
ily—arranged in
a weathered cup-
board, **far right.**

Old leather-bound
books mingle with trea-
sured photos and a
lifetime's collection,
above.

Keep in mind what's
on view when the
doors are open,
right: wicker baskets
help organize
videos and CDs.

Two stacked benches serve as impromptu shelves, holding books and a truckload of CDs.

The view from the living room into the dining room and guest room is enlivened by well-decorated shelves and patterned rugs.

The variety of objects, **above right**, from wicker trays to ironstone compotes to Santa Fe crosses, makes these shelves a museum of my interests.

How It's Done

Start by making piles of the elements you plan to place on the shelves. First, position the largest elements, such as platters and baskets, then add in the books. Because many of my books are oversize, coffee-table volumes, I like to stack them sideways. These stacks make good pedestals for layering objects such as bowls and candlesticks. The key point is not to fill up the whole shelf with books; leave some room for shapelier silhouettes that will break up the monotony. Fill in with pitchers, vases, frames, small statues. (A secret: Not every piece has to be perfect. Place damaged bowls or pitchers that are still lovely to look at on upper shelves, and face the chipped or cracked side toward the wall.) Keep stepping back to get an overall perspective as you proceed, making sure the composition looks balanced.

ABeautifulBath

A painted cabinet with timeworn character softens the shine of a newly tiled bath.

The basic white or beige laminate and acrylic baths in many newer homes may be practical and hygienic, but they often lack warmth or charm. Older baths may have unattractive tiling, poor lighting, exposed plumbing, and little storage. Short of renovation, there are lots of easy ways to make baths old and new look better.

Start with the shower curtain, which in most cases is the largest visible surface in the room. Creating a fabric shower curtain instead of buying one ready-made saves expense and softens the cold look of tile. Hang two curtains instead of one, and have them open in the center, cinched with tiebacks, to frame the tub. Or hang a curtain with a simple valance that goes to the ceiling to give a diminutive bath a sense of grandeur. To counteract an unappealing tile color, choose a lively print—perhaps a vintage fabric (look for old curtains long enough to make into a shower curtain) that complements the bath's coloring but draws attention to itself. Or subdue a strong hue with a simple unbleached linen or canvas curtain. Upgrade from plastic curtain rings to chrome hooks or fabric self-ties. Embroidered bed and table linens, quilt tops, lightweight blankets, and matelassé bedspreads can also make a savvy stand-in for a shower curtain (remember to add a waterproof plastic liner).

Treat the bath as you would a real room. Import good furniture and elegant accessories into the bath: a nice chair or comfy stool; a framed work of art; sconces instead of "bathroom" lighting; silver dresser accessories or pretty perfume flasks. Give character to a new bathroom or add storage to an old one by hanging a painted wood cupboard or set of shelves. If you can't find an antique you like, there are now inexpensive reproduction cabinets with turn-of-the-century charm. Or, if you prefer something with a more modern edge, look for stainless steel or steel cabinets once used in industrial and institutional settings. Instead of a standard medicine chest, hang a beautifully framed mirror and use cupboards for storage. If the bathroom floor is unappealing, rather than using synthetic wall-to-wall bath carpeting, camouflage it with sisal matting, an antique rug, or a large all-cotton bath rug.

An abundance of flowers—on pillows, paintings, pots, and in bloom—and wicker furnishings make this bath, **above,** feel like a secret garden.

The bath often evokes thoughts of the sea, highlighted, **left,** by a silver bowl filled with shells and soap.

A leopard-print stool,
silver and wrought-iron
candlesticks, and
a gilded mirror add
touches of luxe
to a plain white bath.

Natural elegance,
right, comes from a
sink skirted in linen,
a lace tablecloth used
as a shower curtain,
and a burnished
gold mirror.

The beautifully mottled
paint on a cabinet,
above, brings a
textured patina to an
all-white bath.

Intriguing antiques
such as the mirror,
sconces, and paint-
ings, **right,** need
not feel out of place
in the bath.

Towels, hair dryers, soaps, and other bath basics can be stocked out of sight in an old cupboard, **left.**

Sleek brass accents gleam against grass cloth–covered walls, which give warmth to the bath, **center left.**

Wainscoting adds a dash of country charm to any bath; model boats strike a nautical note, **above.**

Twig shutters, a terracotta cup, and an old knife box impart an earthy rusticity to a new bath, **left.**

Silver accessories
from compotes to
cups to filigreed boxes
are an elegant surprise
in a modern-day bath.

Styling Secrets

Quick camouflage:
Hide exposed pipes
beneath a sink with a fabric
skirt, perhaps to match the
shower curtain. Hem two
panels that open in front,
then attach them to the
sink's edge with Velcro.

Stylish storage: Bring in
baskets to hold plump
rolled-up towels, extra rolls
of toilet paper, hair dryer
and brushes, sponges and
soaps. Old knife boxes can
also work as attractive stowaways. The texture of aged
wood and wicker warms up
cold tiled surfaces.

Bring life to the bath:
Plants thrive in the humid
environment, or add color
and fragrance with a vase of
fresh flowers. Light candles
for a romantic glow when
company comes, or just for
yourself when you're relaxing in the tub.

Add luxurious details:
from the plushest towels to
a tortoise-handled tooth-
brush to a silver cup to hold
cotton swabs. Indulge!

TheOrganizedCloset

My treasured collection of concho belts hangs from hooks inside my closet door.

People love to peek into my closets. They will come up with any pretext to get a look at the neat rows of shoes lined up on slim angled shelves (I admit it—I have more pairs than could probably fit in any shoe organizer) and small baskets and trays filled with belts and jewelry. The key to an organized closet in my mind is consistency: I like to have all the same kind of hangers, whether white plastic or wood or wire, and I like to have everything in plain sight (back to the "if you don't see it, you won't use it" rule)—no plastic dry cleaner bags or shoe boxes or opaque storage bins. My closet is divided into city/work clothes and casual/country clothes, and organized by type (jackets, pants, skirts), length, and color. Sweaters (folded on shelves) are separated into heavy and light weight, but otherwise my closet is seasonless: Because I travel so much, I tend to adjust for temperature by layering.

These guidelines may not be what works best for you, but if you consider how you use your closet—how you select clothes to wear, whether you wear some clothes in just one season, whether you ever wear those hats collecting dust on the top shelf—you will have the keys to begin your own reorganization. If space allows, having a mix of shelves and hanging rods is helpful. I have a peg rack and baskets for belts and shallow baskets and drawers for stockings, socks, and underwear. Hooks are another good solution for belts, caps, and bags. I keep much of my jewelry in the bathroom (necklaces on a mini peg rack; earrings and bracelets in small baskets and trays), which helps me remember to wear it. I use glass salt and pepper shakers to store basics like buttons and safety pins. Baskets on the floor of the closet hold laundry and ironing; my suitcases are also stowed on the floor, though some people prefer the top shelf. If you find there are certain clothes or accessories that never seem to have a home, determine what would be the best way to store them (drawers, shelves, hooks, hat boxes, baskets) and make room.

I clean out my closet every six months. If you find it hard to part with clothes, put anything you're not sure about in the back of the closet, and if you have not worn it in another six months, give it away!

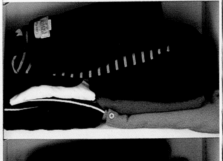

Floor-to-ceiling
angled shelves proffer
shoes at a glance
in my closet, **left;** a
shallow basket holds
belts and scarves.

My Santa Fe closet
is appropriately
Western-themed,
with Native American
photographs and a
Navajo rug, **below.**

Create a closet: An
old blanket chest
keeps Christmas
wraps and decorations
out of sight for the
rest of the year.

Pairs of glasses neatly
lined up on a counter
form an eye-catching
display, **above.**

Above: Cowboy boots are corralled into a neat line along a closet floor. (Stuff socks inside to help them keep their shape.)

A wicker and wood tray, **opposite**, gathers patriotic baubles and glimmering beads for easy access.

Outfitting
A Home Office

Woven baskets,
a coppery cachepot,
even scallop shells
make serendipitous
desk accessories.

Whether you work out of your home, catch up on office projects on your laptop, or just need a quiet place to pay bills and keep up with correspondence, a desk of one's own is finally being appreciated as a necessity in the home. A "home office" might be the kitchen table, a secretary in a corner of the bedroom, a hallway alcove outfitted with a desk, or an entire den or extra bedroom. These days a desk often has to hold more than just pens and papers: It might be home to a computer, fax machine, and printer in addition to the phone, answering machine, and files. Even if it is just a corner of the mudroom, an "office" provides a place to store papers and paraphernalia that could otherwise engulf a house in clutter or get lost in the shuffle. A simple table and comfortable chair, file baskets or drawers, and perhaps a few bookshelves or a bulletin board are the bare basics of what you will need.

While files are often associated with professional offices, I find them indispensable at home for organizing ideas, projects, and documents. I keep folders of everything from articles on travel destinations to owner's manuals for appliances. Most metal file cabinets are too cold and industrial looking for me, so I often use large, shallow wicker baskets and boxes to hold my manila file folders. Catalogs such as Hold Everything now offer wicker file boxes fitted with metal frames for hanging folders; accordion files are also helpful for cataloging papers and receipts.

Beyond file folders, I like to outfit my desk with the same kind of homey touches I use in the rest of the house: Old utensil boxes organize tape, scissors, paper clips, and such; wicker boxes and wooden trays hold papers; silver and horn cups clutch pencils and markers. I see no reason to suddenly settle for plastic and wire in a place where I spend so much of my time. Even in my office away from home, a sisal rug covers up the unattractive industrial carpeting, antique boxes store papers and desk accessories, a big flag hangs on the wall, garden flowers brighten every corner, and a wall-to-wall bulletin board is covered with inspiring pictures and magazine pages, personal photos, and business cards. At home, although I don't have as much room to spread out, my desk is still orga-

With notecards and pens at the ready, **above,** taking care of correspondence becomes much easier.

A memory board made of ribbons tacked into a lattice, **left,** is a picturesque way to hold cards, invitations, and mementos.

An alcove outfitted as a home office, **left,** can be stylishly curtained off when the workday is done.

Vintage straw purses, **below,** make chic and charming catchalls beside a desk.

nized with the same philosophy: An office should be just as appealing and inviting as the rest of the house.

A bulletin board is a helpful catchall for the detritus of daily life—reminders, invitations, newspaper clippings; I also use mine as a visual resource to spark my imagination. Use a standard corkboard, or turn a wall into a bulletin board by nailing up a piece of homosote (available at lumber yards), which can be painted to match the walls. Another, prettier, option: Make a memory board by covering either surface with fabric, then tacking on a lattice of ribbons (tack or staple strips of ribbon diagonally in each direction so they crisscross, then place upholstery or thumbtacks at the intersections); pictures and cards can then be tucked beneath the ribbons. I have an antique wire postcard holder that I hang on the wall to hold treasured cards and mementos; old louvered shutters can also make an unexpected card-holder.

If you want to create privacy or keep work hidden from view, a tall

An old spice cupboard's drawers, **above,** neatly contain odds and ends such as rubber bands, clips, and film.

The rich textures of an embossed leather portfolio and woven baskets, **left,** imbue the everyday with Old World elegance.

folding screen, a floor-to-ceiling curtain, or even a large piece of furniture such as an armoire or bookshelves can help section off an office in an alcove or corner of a room. An infrequently used filing cabinet can be covered with a round wooden top and table skirt to create an instant side table; the desk or a small dining table can be camouflaged with a tailored to-the-floor cloth, with storage space underneath for boxes, books, and projects (protect the top of the tablecloth with a piece of glass cut to the size of the table). Dining rooms often make good office spaces because they are so rarely used for dining. Turn over part of a buffet or sideboard to household records and stationery and use the table as your desk.

The key is not to be limited by ready-made concepts of "office" furniture and desk accessories, but instead to adapt the kind of furnishings you already own to a new role.

155

Open Shelves and
KitchenStowaways

Glass-front cabinets
put china on show;
a ship model is an
unexpected touch on
a countertop.

For decades, the trend in kitchen design was to hide everything away behind opaque banks of kitchen cabinet doors, leaving wide-open expanses of bare countertop, but that's never really been my style. I thrive on having a well-organized kitchen, but I much prefer to have things out in plain view, where I can appreciate their utilitarian beauty and have instant access to them. No one has ever had to ask, "Where are the bowls?" in my kitchen—they can just help themselves.

That is not to say everything should be out in the open: Cabinets are wonderful for protecting fragile wares and hiding the less aesthetic necessities, such as foodstuffs and pots and pans. But I have always tried to have as much open shelving as possible for displaying (and storing) platters, bowls, plates, pitchers, glassware, cookbooks, and more. I also believe in having cooking tools and utensils readily at hand, so my counters are lined with bottles of oils and vinegars, cups and crocks filled with wooden spoons and wire whisks, jars of condiments and bottles of spices. I often even keep flatware out in a cutlery box or divided basket, which makes it easy to set the table or grab a spoon when I need it. This out-of-the-closet philosophy brings a kitchen to life, while also serving very practical needs.

There are plenty of places in which to tuck in extra shelves in a kitchen—above the sink or stove (allow room for venting), across an unused wall, in a mudroom or entry area, above an eating nook or table (at picture rail height). Or you may be able to convert some of your cabinetry into open shelving simply by removing the cabinet doors. Remove the door hardware and fill holes with wood putty; then paint or finish the insides and outsides of cabinets to match. You can also update cabinets by having new doors—glass-fronted or otherwise—installed, for much less money than it would cost to replace the cabinetry. Using pieces of furniture such as cupboards, hutches, and armoires in the kitchen—in addition to or in place of cabinets—is another more inviting way to provide storage. The homey warmth of "unfitted" kitchens of the past is coming back into appreciation.

A stainless-steel ledge and stove-side peg racks keep condiments and cutlery handy, **left.** (Note the swing-arm faucet on the stove for filling large pots.)

An old crock is put into service holding an array of utensils, **above.**

Shelves and walls have a monochromatic simplicity painted in soothing sage green, **left.**

One wall of my cottage kitchen is lined with white shelves, providing open-air access to platters, bowls, and glassware.

A large pot rack with adjustable hooks, **above,** makes good use of above-counter space in a small kitchen.

Wooden dish-drying racks, hung on the wall, can also be used to store plates and platters, **right.**

Old shelves and planks lined with hooks hold copper pots in a pantry-style kitchen, **left.**

An iron display stand, **above,** creates free-standing storage while showing off china.

A collection of majolica pitchers, **left,** is a charming way to hold wooden spoons and serving utensils.

Test tubes in a rack make ideal spice jars, **above,** keeping limited quantities fresh and at hand.

I've devoted shelves to entertaining supplies, **right,** from wicker bottles to crystal decanters.

Styling Secrets

Quick and easy ways to add open storage to your kitchen (and put empty wall space to work):

Hang an old-fashioned plate rack (an easily accessible way to store large platters and trays), a rack for wineglasses, or a dish-drying rack above the sink.

Install hooks or a peg rack to keep utensils, dish towels, and pot holders near at hand.

Add a pot rack (or large hooks) by the stove or above an island to house pots and pans.

Use hanging wire baskets to hold fruits and vegetables aloft.

Add cup hooks to the undersides of shelves to expand their storage potential.

Hang pretty platters and plates on the wall when they are not in use.

On counters, on shelves, and within cabinets, use baskets and trays to help organize smaller items such as dish towels, condiments, and cutlery. Baskets can even be used inside the refrigerator to store basics such as eggs and cheese.

My new Santa Fe home offered an opportunity to put all my favorite quick decorating ideas into practice.

Putting It All Together

Now you know all my secrets—the quick tricks that make rooms look more lush and inviting and make each house feel like a well-loved home. But how do you make it all work together, or what if you are starting from scratch? In this chapter I will explain the overall process, start to finish, using my new adobe house in Santa Fe as a case study. We photographed the whole thing step by step as I moved in.

So often people tell me that they have been living in their home for several years or more and still have not furnished it the way they would like, or hung pictures on the wall, or put curtains at the windows. My philosophy is that life is too short to waste years worrying about decorating. I put together my new house in Santa Fe literally in four days. By the end of the week, if you had stopped by, you probably would have thought I had lived there for years. Yes, I did some advance planning and shopping in the month beforehand, but that can be helpful even when you are not on a deadline. So what are you waiting for? Now is the time to take care of those details and start enjoying your home.

Starting Fresh

The only way to stay sane during a move is to make lists, and check them twice.

Much of what makes decorating quicker and easier is streamlining the decision-making process. Instead of agonizing over upholstery fabrics and window treatments, or rethinking my whole scheme each time I move, I rely on certain basics: overstuffed white sofas; the simplest white curtains; painted antique furniture; peg racks on the wall; Navajo rugs or sisal matting on the wood floors; white walls (no need to worry about paint colors); my collections of American country furniture, Native American textiles, blue willow china, and black-and-white photographs. The furniture may move around, the accessories may change, but the basic core remains much the same.

This scheme is adaptable to a surprisingly wide variety of settings. From a modern SoHo loft to shingled beach cottages to my latest acquisition, a Santa Fe adobe house, my "cleaned-up country" decorating style and favorite pieces have worked in every home. Most of the furnishings now in Santa Fe were in my New York apartment or Hamptons beach house and they made the cross-country and cross-culture transition effortlessly. What changed were the accent pieces: The city architectural prints and seaside paraphernalia stayed home, and out came all my favorite Southwest collectibles: carved Mexican crosses and religious icon paintings, Indian blankets and Navajo rugs, tinware, and turquoise-studded silver accessories. Suddenly, the same white sofas and painted cupboards took on a Southwestern air.

Your furniture will certainly be different from mine, but if you select high-quality basics in classic shapes, you will have made a good investment. You may outgrow your passion for floral chintz or stain your pale gray armchairs, but if the sofa and chairs have clean, simple lines, all you have to do is slipcover them when it is time for a change. Save to invest in good pieces, rather than buying slipshod "starter" furniture in quantity, or buy secondhand and trade up to better quality as you can afford to. Think also in terms of pieces that can serve multiple purposes: tables that can work as a desk, hall table, or small kitchen table; chairs that can pull up to the dining table or stand alone; armoires and cupboards that can serve as

Save all receipts
and bills in a special
folder or envelope
in case anything
breaks or must
be returned, **below.**

Clip magazines and
catalogs, **above,** for
design inspiration, or
for furnishings you're
interested in buying.

Left: Do what the
pros do: Bring a cam-
era when shopping
to snap photos of pos-
sibilities; then sort
through them in situ
to see what selection
will work best.

dressers, pantries, entertainment cabinets, or bars. These adaptable workhorses will no doubt find a place in any home you own. Good outdoor wicker or iron furniture can also do double duty, pinch-hitting indoors in casual rooms when needed. Accessories such as mirrors, lamps, and rugs can be chosen with the same eye toward versatility.

When you are about to move into a new home, the first thing is to get the "backgrounds" right. Have walls and ceilings patched and painted, and floors refinished; do any necessary repairs to moldings, windows, or tile; and install light fixtures. If these fundamentals are not attended to before moving day, they usually never get done at all.

There are some exceptions to the do-it-all-right-away rule, however. If you are wavering about a detail, it makes sense to live with it for a while. I originally planned to paint out the gold-colored moldings in the living room, but when the room was all done, with a few furnishings and accents picking up on the gold, I decided the moldings truly suited the room, so I left them as is.

Once the "canvas" is clean, it is easier to assess a room's strengths (large windows, a fireplace, spacious layout) and weaknesses (a view of a brick wall, inadequate light, an awkward layout). Draw up a floor plan of your home roughly to scale, and make several photocopies to make it easier to plan out possible room arrangements. Measure everything, including doorways, so you will know whether or not your furniture fits through the door and within each room. Those measurements are also essential to have with you when you are shopping.

With my floor plan in hand, I assessed the pieces I already owned to see what would work in the new house. My friend Carol Glasser also generously combed through her own extra furnishings for candidates for my home. Once I had figured out what I could use that I already owned (a sofa and club chairs, dining chairs and a table, various rugs and pictures, and plenty of accessories), and what Carol could donate (two twin French beds, some damask chairs), I began shopping for pieces to fill the "holes" (a double bed, a table for the kitchen, side tables, a few more lamps and chairs). I had new furnishings shipped directly from stores to my new address (which saved on sales tax, not to mention hassles). Then, the big move began.

While furnishings are still wrapped (and protected), move them around to find the best placement.

Ground zero: Start by unpacking items into the rooms where they belong, **left.**

Help is always welcome: Our intrepid handyman, Andy Bennivedes, **above,** lent a hand unpacking.

One problem I didn't anticipate: The moving van could not fit in my small street, so everything had to be reloaded into a smaller truck, **left.**

ARoomforLiving

Before: The basic pieces of furniture are in place; baskets holding linens and accessories will soon become "tables."

The living room is typically the largest, most well-designed room in the house, so it is usually the focus of the most decorating attention. Rather than signaling "don't touch," it should feature comfortable seating, a coffee table that can stand having feet rested on it, and ample chairs for entertaining. I love a living room that invites "living," a comfortable area in which to read, work, or listen to music.

For the layout of the room, the most important considerations are the traffic flow, the focal points, and the various functions the room will serve. Many rooms suggest a natural arrangement based on built-in elements like windows and doors, a fireplace, or bookshelves. For example, a classic arrangement in a living room with a fireplace is to have a sofa facing the fireplace with chairs on either side, or to have two sofas (or a sofa and two chairs, as I did) facing each other, perpendicular to the fireplace. But you may prefer to float a grouping in the center of the room, particularly in the summer, when the fireplace is not being used. If the room does not have a focus, you can create one, such as a large painting or a collection grouped on one wall, a massive Welsh cupboard filled with colorful plates, a grand mirror or dramatic quilt hung above a sofa. Consider what will be seen when visitors first enter the room, and make sure that it is worthy of the attention. Also take a look at the room from adjacent rooms and doorways, and note what will be in the line of vision. Views from room to room have a surprising amount of impact. You do not want to obstruct views or traffic flow with either large or fragile pieces of furniture. If the living room will be used for writing letters or paying bills, find a place for a desk along one wall or in a corner. If it will serve as a playroom for children, allow floor space for them. If it will be a second—or the only—dining room, add a drop-leaf table or choose a coffee table that is a few inches higher to make dining easier. If it is where you will do most of your entertaining, assign a cupboard, tray table, or shelves in a closet for a bar.

In Santa Fe, along one wall of the living room, I flanked the doorway to the dining room/library with a writing table and a buffet topped with

bar accessories. On the opposite wall, a large armoire houses the television and stereo in comfortable proximity to the sofa. The upholstered chairs can be swiveled around for television viewing, if needed, but most of the time they form a cozy seating group around the wicker coffee table (sizable enough to hold drinks and hors d'oeuvres). Side chairs can easily be drawn up to expand seating.

A room's deficiencies can often be turned into assets. An awkward nook might be just the place to seclude a desk, or you could shelve it and create storage for your stereo. Small rooms can often benefit by being made to feel cozy, filled with rich patterns and colors and lots of books, rather than being left spare. If windows look out onto an unattractive view, dress them in sheer scrim panels to let in light while obscuring the view, or use shutters or curtains if light is not important. A small window could even be fitted with glass shelves to display plants or a collection. If the shape of the room or the placement of doorways creates awkward

After: Furniture is arranged to bask in the glow of the fire; a massive armoire adds height and grandeur.

171

The base of a wicker chaise makes a generous coffee table, on which I've started trying out candlesticks and vases.

traffic patterns, flexibility becomes essential: Use light, movable chairs rather than large, bulky upholstered pieces, and versatile tray or stacking tables instead of a huge coffee table. Put the television on a wheeled stand so it can be tucked away when not in use.

The entire room need not be planned out on paper first, of course. Often the best way to create an arrangement is to just start moving the furniture around. The most common mistakes are lining up all the furniture against the walls or, conversely, pushing seating too close together. Create an open, loosely defined seating area in the center of the room or oriented toward a focal point; an area rug can help to define it. In a larger room, you can create more than one seating or work area. Give space to each piece of furniture, while maintaining a relationship between them: Too many cupboards or tables cannot be appreciated individually, and the end result will look cluttered. Small occasional tables should be paired with chairs or sofas; spare chairs can flank an armoire or doorway, or pull up to a table. After the basic arrangement is in place, stand back and take in the overall effect from various vantage points. Once you are pleased with the result (and it should never be set in stone anyway), move the furniture away and lay down any rugs. These should be large enough to encompass the furniture, but small enough to show a border of floor.

Your furniture may be a mix of antique and new, family hand-me-downs, and flea-market finds. What makes it all work together successfully is a similarity of scale and style, with some consistency of color and pattern. That doesn't mean everything should match—just the opposite is true—but proportions should be harmonious. Slipcovers can unify disparate chairs and upholstered pieces, or help them make the transition to a new setting. I cloaked my dining chairs with red-checked seats in natural linen slipcovers with skirts to the floor, and suddenly they had enough sophistication to sit in the living room (though most of them ended up around the kitchen table). Short, tailored seat covers dressed down gilded velvet chairs to help them blend with my canvas-covered sofa and chairs. But keep in mind that contrast is what gives a room life, and juxtapositions of style can be surprisingly successful. My friend Carol's statuesque blue damask chairs were dramatically different from my casual canvas seating, but I think they help bridge the elegance of the

room with the more down-to-earth furnishings. On the other hand, if all the furniture were dark, tapestry-covered antiques, the room would become too formal and forbidding. The contrast in coloring also helps energize the room: The dark wood tables, desk, lamps, and candlesticks create elegant silhouettes against the parchment walls and ivory slipcovers. The touch of French blue in the chairs picks up on the blue stripes in the dhurrie rug, while the wicker table and baskets enhance the textural mix.

Another hint: Don't ignore the corners. Instead of leaving them for dead, light them with standing lamps, sconces, or uplighting; hang a picture or mirror on one wall; place a large plant on a pedestal or stand a tree in a corner. Corner cupboards are another useful solution, or nestle shelves, a round table, or the television into a corner. The desk and bar in this room helped create cozy niches in two of the corners, and standing candlesticks help light the other two.

The armoire is centered beneath the dramatic peak of the ceiling; sets of chairs echo this symmetry.

One niche flanking the living room entry was the perfect size for an English walnut buffet, which became home to an impromptu bar.

Lighting is an essential element that is often overlooked. Make sure there is adequate lighting by each seating area, on desks and over tables. There should be a mix of task lighting—table and standing lamps—as well as ambient lighting from overhead fixtures and wall sconces. The rule of thumb is five to seven sources of light in a room—a standard woefully few rooms meet. The element that makes the single biggest difference in the quality of light is a dimmer switch, to control the level of light, especially important for overhead and track lighting. There is a good deal of natural light in my living room, thanks to several sets of French doors. To the numerous pairs of sconces already in the room, I added a reading lamp behind one chair, table lamps on the desk and chest, and, of course, lots of candles. The overall effect is of a warm, golden glow, with more direct pools of light where needed.

Pictures and window treatments should be the last elements added to the room. In fact, no art should be hung until everything else, including the accessories, has found a place. Then prop up pictures first, if possible, to see how they work. If you're unsure about the length or style of curtains, these too could be tacked into place until you get a feel for the quality of light in the room. I propped up a Mexican religious icon painting on the bar and hung a framed mirror just above the writing table. Black-and-white photographs did not seem rich enough for this location, but some gold-framed Raphael prints I had in storage from a previous apartment fit the bill perfectly. I hung them just above two stacked wicker chests between the French doors.

The small touches that helped finish the room—fresh flowers, stacks of books, the fringed wool throw over the chair, vignettes with baskets, candles and other collectibles—are just the kinds of decorative elements we have been exploring in previous chapters. To my all-purpose favorites, I added elements native to Santa Fe: carved religious statues (*santos*), paintings, and crosses.

I knew this was a room I could live in happily when we watched the Academy Awards telecast while eating take-out pizza and drinking champagne (thoughtful housewarming gestures from my friend and neighbor, Peter Vitale) the first night I moved in, surrounded by half-unpacked boxes. It hasn't disappointed yet.

The other niche
was filled with a
carved Mexican desk
and became a snug
corner for writing.

Create a Living

Room in 3 Hours

Pairs of sconces flank the doorway, fireplace, windows, and armoire, gently washing light across the weathered walls.

A chest tucked into a corner niche is set up with bar accoutrements for easy entertaining.

Two engravings are hung just above the stacked wicker trunks; the mirror and *santos* painting are also set low.

Within easy reach of the sofa is a small side table for holding drinks and whatnot.

A white canvas sofa offers crisp contrast to the dark woods, and is well positioned to enjoy both the fire and a television hidden in the armoire.

Casablanca lilies, heightened by a stack of books, have a strong presence to catch the eye.

A blue-and-white-striped dhurrie adds a pleasing note of color to a predominantly neutral room.

A Dining Room
ThatDoesMore

The shelf-lined entry-way seemed just large enough to hold a dining table, making optimum use of the space.

Few of us sit down to a formal meal around a dining table every night anymore. We still cook, have family meals, and even entertain on occasion, but in more informal and impromptu ways. As a result, the dining room has become a ghost room in many homes. In many newer houses, dining areas are combined with the kitchen and family room as part of a great room. But if you have a separate dining room, as most homes still do, it is wise to find ways to get more use from the space. If you wish to use it as a home office, cupboards and armoires can store faxes and files as easily as china and crystal. Dining tables that can be shortened or extended with leaves or drop-leaf sides lend themselves to greater functionality. With a compacted table, you may have room for a comfortable reading chair in an alcove, or a computer table that can be rolled away or hidden behind a screen when not in use. You may decide to turn a sunroom or solarium into a cozy dining room, or use your kitchen for family meals and set up living-room buffets for entertaining, freeing up your dining room for a study, music room, or guest room.

My Santa Fe house had no formal dining room, but I decided to make its gracious shelf-lined entry hall into a combination library and dining room. You could also turn a dining room into a library by lining one or more walls with books. I love the warm familiarity of entertaining all my guests around one table, so I was happy to find a place for my refectory table, to which I can pull up chairs when needed. Dining chairs need not all match—in fact, it makes for a livelier mix to have an assortment of several styles, perhaps all of the same wood or painted the same color. Because my dining room is not large and serves as a passageway, I kept the chairs to a minimum, but eight chairs can easily fit around the table for dinner. Chairs do not always need to stand at attention around a dining table. Place some along the walls, flanking a sideboard or doorway, or set below a pair of sconces.

My black-and-white photographs of Georgia O'Keeffe's home in Abiquiu, New Mexico, taken by Myron Wood, did not look appropriate in the living room, but they suited the crisp white walls of the dining

room, so they now frame its French doors. Taking a tip from photographer Bruce Weber, I zigzagged a series of small Navajo rugs across the dining room's brick floor, ending with a blue-and-white striped rug that visually connects with the rug in the adjoining living room.

I exchanged the delicate chandelier that had been in the dining room for a heftier, more rustic one in wrought iron. The dining room is one place where the lighting absolutely should be on a dimmer switch. Or supplant it entirely with candlelight: Stately silver candlesticks and a candelabra in the corner stand at the ready for romantic dinners.

The spirit of the dining room is conviviality, and the few simple elements required—table, chairs, perhaps a cupboard—should be chosen to make guests feel at home. A dining room can be a simple canvas embellished by food, flowers, candlelight, smiling faces, and generous laughter.

Filled with beautiful china, books, and pictures, the dining hall invites guests to linger.

Create a Dining

Room in 2 Hours

Instead of filling shelves with only china or wall-to-wall volumes, a rich mix of wicker baskets, blue-and-white platters, and bite-size servings of books makes for a livelier menu.

Statuesque silver candelabra are all that's needed to light intimate dinners; a chandelier offers more controlled illumination.

A large flowering plant nestled inside a basket brings a sign of life to the room.

The narrow refectory table doesn't overwhelm a limited space; extra chairs can be borrowed from the kitchen and living room and pulled up as needed.

Charming frame-backed chairs are pulled up to the table informally, as if in conversation, rather than in a lifeless lineup.

Navajo rugs a bit small for the space are overlapped, building up pattern and length.

KitchenCentral

White cabinets, beige tiles, and natural slip-covers create a neutral base in the kitchen.

If our dining rooms are doing less, our kitchens are doing more. True to the old adage that guests always seem to end up in the kitchen, it is becoming the center of the home again as it was a century ago. Some people incorporate sitting areas, home offices, greenhouses, or entertainment centers into their kitchens. At the very least, it is nice to have a dining table in the kitchen for homework, bill-paying, and casual family meals. I bought an oval antique table in Texas to set before the kitchen hearth (one of the charms of this Santa Fe home is that there is a fireplace in every room). Oval tables are hard to find, but they are ideal when space is limited; they do not take up as wide a circumference as a round table, but the rounded edges make it easier to slide by in a high-traffic area like the kitchen. Oval-backed chairs with red-and-white checked upholstery, formerly used in the dining area of my loft, were slipcovered in simple single-pleat skirts to suit the informality of the kitchen. A Velcro panel at the base of the chair back gives the covers a better fit. To-the-floor slipcovers would not be a good choice with children, but I liked the versatility they offered: These chairs can move into the dining room or living room with ease.

By painting the cabinets creamy white and changing the green backsplash tile to a light-expanding beige, I allowed my accessories to add color and interest. Given a choice, I would have selected white fronts rather than black for the appliances, but I minimized them by adding visual excitement elsewhere. Though there were more cabinets than I like to have, I was able to simulate the feel of open shelving by lining the tops of cabinets with blue-and-white spongeware mixing bowls, and populating the countertops with platters, baskets, bowls, and crocks of utensils. These created the sense of accessibility that I prefer in a kitchen.

For the fireplace mantel, I created a still life from white ironstone pottery—pitchers, cake stands, and candlesticks—filled with fresh touches of white and green, in flowers, artichokes, and limes, all picked up at a nearby grocery store. Along with the bowls brimming with fruit on the table, these final touches are what say "I'm home" to me.

A collection of white ironstone china filled with crisp green fruits and flowers brightens the kitchen hearth, **above.**

A gleaming copper fish poacher filled with oils and condiments, **left,** is an unexpected route to countertop organization.

Cozy Up a

Kitchen in 2½ Hours

Good task lighting is essential for preparing a meal; here, simple track lights do the job unobtrusively.

Blue-and-white spongeware bowls, enlivening the cabinet-to-ceiling gap, are old country friends that always feel at home in a kitchen.

A table lamp is a surprising, yet homey, touch on a counter.

Counters and ledges filled with baskets, platters, and bowls make the room feel warm and lived-in.

Cabinets were painted creamery white, and sand-toned tile was installed to keep the kitchen light and airy.

Bowls brimming with fruit are a bright spot in a neutral kitchen, and create an instant sense of bounty.

Brick floors, typical of an adobe home, are sturdy, but can tire the feet. Place area rugs by the sink and other workstations.

ABedroomRefuge

Softly ruffled shams, a piqué bedspread, and Marseilles skirt add pure white elegance to the bed.

The bedroom is our personal space in a home; it should be a place of comfort and serenity. In addition to the bed, which should be the best quality affordable (I wish I had learned earlier in life to invest in down pillows!), and a bureau or armoire, it is nice to have a comfortable reading chair or chaise, and perhaps a desk or dressing table, if there is room. The bed, usually placed with the headboard against a wall (though it does not have to be), should be oriented to catch a breeze from the windows and the light in the morning. However, in many bedrooms limited size restricts the bed to one location. Place necessary comforts within easy reach: good reading lights on each side of the bed and small tables or chests for clock, tissues, books, and glasses. Area rugs or carpeting can help take the chill off early-morning awakenings, and blinds, shades or curtains should provide privacy and darkness when desired. Choose window treatments that allow control over the level of light: Roman shades or wooden blinds can be tucked beneath curtains to offer more flexibility.

Make room for adequate storage in the bedroom, so clothes and accessories have a home; nothing is less relaxing than looking at clutter. If closets are small, a chest at the end of the bed, underbed boxes, or wicker trunks stacked on a wall can help supplement storage. Most important, carve out room for the things that mean most to you—personal photographs and mementos, favorite books or collections.

My master bedroom in Santa Fe was filled with ready-made charms: a window seat tucked beneath casement windows that look out on the garden, a cozy fireplace to warm up cool nights, and built-in niches and shelves to house books and other belongings. I added a cache of striped, plaid, and floral pillows to the plain window-seat cushion, and since the alcove seemed a little bare, I brought in a wicker chair from the porch and laid down a Navajo rug. A white armchair and ottoman provide a comfy spot to curl up by the fire with a good book or a glass of wine. My mannequin lamp, now modeling a fringed leather jacket and beads, provided lighting with personality. I found a painted French headboard in one store in Houston and I found the similarly curvaceous bedside

An assortment of
blanket-plaid and vin-
tage floral pillows, a
Navajo rug, and extra
chairs cozy up the
window-seat corner.

chests in another. The Mexican tin lamps, picked up in a shop near
Santa Fe, now have black shades instead of white, which I think looks
much richer. In crisp contrast to the furniture, I kept the linens all
white but added subtle texture with a piqué bedspread, Marseilles bedskirt, and ruffled pillow shams.

In the guest bedroom's smaller quarters, I tucked in Carol's two charming single beds, which had lines similar to those of my bed. My Beacon
blankets and vintage curtains (which I plan to have made into duvet covers) serendipitously picked up the red of the bed frames. The color warms
the white ruffled linens that continue in this room. Since space was at a
premium, I slipped in slender modern lamps beside each bed, and the
tiled windowsill serves as a bedside perch. Even in a diminutive guest-
room, thoughtful touches such as fresh flowers and towels, a stock of cur-
rent magazines, and fragrant toiletries will offer a warm welcome.

A windowed alcove
that overlooks the gar-
den welcomes light
into the bedroom and
makes a natural spot
for seating.

Charm a Bed

room in an Hour

If the view is private, there's no need to block pretty casement windows with curtains, unless you want to control the light.

In a room where every inch counts, slim standing lamps (or wall sconces) take up little space.

Flowers transport the scent and beauty of the garden indoors.

The charming curlicues of painted headboards are shown to advantage against spare white walls.

Similarly, the pleated flange of a delicate white pillow sham stands out against the red headboard.

Color unites differing textiles—Beacon blankets and vintage floral curtains (which will be made into duvet covers).

When you don't want to bother with bedskirts, cover the boxspring with a fitted sheet.

189

BathinginLuxury

Above: A ladderback chair becomes a convenient repository for beads and bracelets.

The bath, whether a master bath, guest bath, or powder room, should be a haven of sensory pleasures: soft towels, scented lotions and bath powders, flickering candlelight. I found my brick-floored bath to be a little cold, so I warmed it with a Navajo rug, textured baskets, sepia-toned photographs (old Edward Curtis prints I cut out of a book), and silver dresser accessories atop an impromptu table fashioned from an old pantry bucket which once sat next to my sofa. A mirror from my beach cottage happened to fit perfectly between the bath's sconces, and I used a basket filled with makeup and toiletries to camouflage an awkward sliver of marble countertop in the corner. The front of the counter could be skirted; right now I have a large wicker laundry hamper beneath it. Scented candles create a soothing glow for nighttime soaks.

I know I will continue to change and add pieces to my lovely adobe, tweaking the mix just a little bit with each visit—it's in my nature. But I was pleased to realize just how quickly (four exhausting but satisfying days) I could make my new house feel truly like a home. I hope it will inspire you to do the same!

An awkward niche, **right,** is warmed by a toiletry-filled wicker basket, votive candles and sconces, and a sepia print.

Living room elements—sconces, an Indian rug, framed photographs, and a chair—introduce comfort into the bathroom.

100 Quick Tips

Moving In

Here are some of the strategies I've learned over dozens of moves to make the whole process less painful:

1 Label all boxes and bags so movers will know to which room they go and you know where to find things easily. Give movers a floor plan with the location of furniture marked on it.

2 Pack soft furnishings—linens, pillows, slipcovers—in trash bags. Pack toiletries in plastic resealable bags so if they break, they won't spill onto everything.

3 If you can, borrow moving boxes from a friend who's just moved. On the other end, hire a young kid to break down boxes for recycling.

4 Mark an "Open First" box with toolbox, scissors, phone, alarm clock, lightbulbs, and other things you'll need immediately.

5 Send your suitcases ahead via UPS (remember to lock them).

6 Hire someone to clean the house ahead of time so you can start unpacking right away.

7 Go to the grocery store near your new home when you first arrive, because you won't get a chance to later. Get cleaning supplies, trash bags, comfort food. Buy plastic cups, plates, and utensils to use until everything's unpacked and cleaned.

8 Hang a garbage bag on the door of each room as you pack and unpack so you can throw out unneeded items and packing materials.

9 Hold on to all receipts until you are sure nothing is missing or damaged. Keep them in a "moving" folder with closing papers, important phone numbers, to-do lists. Make notes as you unpack of what you need to buy or do.

10 As you unpack glasses and plates, load them into the dishwasher to get rid of any stains or dust from newspaper or packing materials. Hand wash large platters and bowls, and put them upside down on big beach towels to dry. Put silver that needs to be polished in a basket to do later. Wash or dry-clean slipcovers, curtains, and bed linens.

11 When you have finally finished unpacking, fill bowls and vases with fruits and flowers and put candles in candlesticks—it will make you feel at home.

Keep a Stylist's Kit

12 Make a kit of utility items you cannot live without as you set up or organize a home. Put it all in a fanny pack and you won't have to keep looking for things! In my kit, I have:

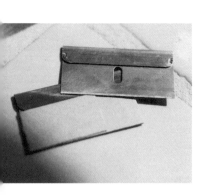

- Oops!, a solvent that's great for removing price stickers, and a single-edge razor blade to do the same
- a utility knife or penknife for opening boxes
- pushpins, which come in handy for tacking up curtains or fabric, putting up wreaths and holiday decorations, holding display plates in place, and a multitude of other contingencies
- straight pins and safety pins for anchoring fabric
- Krazy Glue
- Ticky Tack, a putty-like substance that holds plates or other objects in place without harming walls or surfaces
- Ziploc resealable bags for organizing small items in a tool box, sewing kit, or kitchen drawer
- masking tape and gaffer's (wide black cloth) tape, which will hold almost anything in place
- an assortment of scissors, for flower cutting, paper, kitchen tasks
- a measuring tape, which comes in handy while hanging pictures, making sure furniture will fit, and measuring for drapes. I keep one with me at all times
- wire for hanging pictures or jury-rigging items
  And of course, keep your toolbox handy, outfitted with screwdrivers, hammer, nails, pliers, drill, extension cords, etc.

Shopping

13 Take Polaroids (or many stores will take them for you) of items you're thinking about buying so you can remember them clearly when you are at home.

14 Keep floor plans and measurements of rooms, windows, and other features with you so when you spot "the perfect piece" you will know whether or not it will really work in the space.

15 You can usually buy antiques on approval so that you can take them home and see if they work well in the space before you commit to a purchase. Don't hesitate to return furniture if you get it home and it doesn't suit your space.

16 If you don't have a ruler or measuring tape handy (for example, at a flea market), use a dollar bill—it measures 6 inches long.

17 Be sure to purchase rug pads for area rugs: It will keep them from slipping, extend their wear, and make them softer to walk on.

Decorating

18 Instead of stripping and refinishing furniture that is not high-quality, it's much easier to paint it instead.

19 Chairs can be used for more than seating: Use them as side tables, to stack books on, or as an impromptu easel for artwork.

20 Benches are another must-have. Use one next to a bathtub for books and toiletries, next to a chair for a side table, or to give height to a display. Stack several benches to form bookshelves.

21 Turn a bench into an ottoman by padding it and covering it with fabric. Secure with upholstery tacks.

22 Attractive door stops are hard to find. Consider using large shells, cowboy boots, or a watering can filled with sand.

23 If your sisal rug has seen better days, paint it with marine paint and use it on the porch.

24 An old ladder can become a display space or narrow shelving

when anchored against a wall. Leaned against a wall, the ladder can become an additional towel rack or quilt rack.

25 Lamps can be created from almost any sturdy base—a salvaged baluster, cast-iron urn, wire topiary form, alabaster vase, large wooden candlestick, art pottery or earthenware crock, china teapot, country birdhouse, watering can, even a dressmaker's mannequin.

26 Personalize plain ready-made lampshades with old photographs or slides, by covering them in wallpaper or fabric, or trimming them with rawhide stitching or fringe. They can also be hand-cut in stenciled patterns, papered in old maps or blueprints, decorated with découpaged or rubber-stamped motifs, or covered in artificial rosebuds.

27 If your rugs are too short or small for a room, try zigzagging several across the floor.

28 Hide stains on upholstery with blankets or throws.

29 Tack up fabric shades or curtains with brass upholstery tacks for a speedy alternative to hanging them on rods.

30 Make a quick romantic canopy with mosquito netting. Or hang two large curtains or swaths of fabric above the bed, and drape to each side by tucking them behind curtain bosses or holdbacks.

31 Tuck vintage tablecloths or linens between the mattress and boxspring to create an impromptu dust ruffle. Or wrap the boxspring in an old blanket or coverlet.

32 Think about how the insides of cabinets look—especially if it's a cabinet that's frequently open, like an armoire with a television or stereo.

33 Save shards of broken pottery and china, if they were pieces you loved, and use them to cover a tabletop or planter (glue on pieces and fill in with grout). You can do the same thing with favorite stones, shells, seaglass, or arrowheads.

34 If people ask what you want for gifts, ask several friends to pool their resources for one good thing—better to have one nice platter than five $20 ones. Or let them know what you collect and where to find it

—antique silverware, Russel Wright pottery, Pendleton blankets—so you'll get something you really love.

35 Don't save things, use them!

Candles

36 Buy candles by the dozen (or more)—in votives, tapers, and pillars. That way you'll always have a ready supply for entertaining.

37 To make candles last longer, freeze them ahead of time.

38 To remove wax from the bottom of votives or candlesticks, put them in the freezer, then remove wax with a dull knife.

39 Remove all traces of wax before putting glass votives in the dishwasher; otherwise, wax can melt and stop up the drain.

40 Use dripless candles in sconces and chandeliers.

41 Don't let candles in wooden candlesticks burn down to the bottom, or they can singe the wood.

42 To remove wax from tablecloths or other surfaces, scrape off as much as possible with a credit card or dull knife. Then place several paper towels on top of the drip, and iron over it on low heat, replacing with clean towels as needed.

43 Wrap candle ends in foil to make them fit snugly into candleholders.

Flowers and Fruits

44 Plant just one bulb in a small container, such as an old silver cigarette urn.

45 As roses die, save the petals in a small bowl so you can enjoy their scent after their bloom has faded.

46 If you don't have time to buy flowers or plants, just let your onions go to seed—they'll start sprouting in every direction.

47 Use a zester to peel spirals out of lemons, limes, and oranges for a pretty bar or table decoration.

48 If topiaries have dried up and died, you can spray them with green florist's paint—or leave them as is and enjoy their sculptural beauty.

49 To age terra-cotta pots, spread yogurt or buttermilk on them and leave outside in the shade until they start to get mossy.

50 Fill a clear glass vase with cranberries or limes instead of marbles to hold flowers in place.

51 Top plant pots with moss—it looks prettier than dirt.

52 Artificial flowers are getting better and better looking. Keep some on hand for when you can't get to the flower market.

53 Pretty placecard ideas: Spell out (short) names in cloves on an orange to make a personalized pomander. Write names on shells, then save in a bowl as a remembrance of dinner parties. Pen names with a gold metallic marker on leaves.

Pictures and Frames

54 Change the photographs in your picture frames every so often, so you appreciate them anew.

55 Make black-and-white photostats of your photos to frame. It will preserve the original, and makes a color picture look older and more interesting.

56 Buy plain black frames from the five-and-ten (they're incredibly cheap) and fill them with family photographs or old postcards and use them to cover a wall in a hallway or bath.

57 Paint inexpensive wood frames silver or gold to make them look more elegant.

58 Leave a favorite picture book open to a different page every week to enjoy, instead of storing it away on a shelf. Use a magnifying glass, a cross, a stone, or other memento as a weight to hold the pages open.

59 To make a more sophisticated bulletin board, cover cork with velvet or other fabric and put it inside a large gilded frame.

60 Keep favorite photos tucked into your date book, where you can enjoy them.

Organizing

61 Streamline your belongings and purchases to make things easier to organize or replace: buy all white towels, white plates, white plastic hangers.

62 It sounds obvious, but store things near where you need them: Barbecue equipment and sports gear should go in the mud room or in a cabinet or closet near the door; put things you don't use often in high or less accessible cabinets; keep platters for entertaining and party goods together; store plates and silverware near the kitchen table or dining room (some people prefer to keep them close to the dishwasher).

63 Keep a trash basket by the front door or wherever you open your mail, and immediately discard junk mail, circulars, and extraneous material in bills.

64 Keep a page-a-day calendar or large daily planner. As you receive invitations, tickets, or bills, tuck them into the day when you need to pay, order, or use them. Write everyone's birthdays for the year in your calendar, or note them a few days ahead of time so you'll remember to send a card or buy a gift.

65 Store sugar, flour, pasta, and other dry foods in canisters, where they'll stay fresher and pests can't get to them. Keep eggs and cheeses in a basket in the refrigerator.

66 Use wooden spring clothespins to keep bags of potato chips and bread tightly closed.

67 Rely on trays to organize jars or utensils in the kitchen, to hold glasses on a bar, to hold jewelry and toiletries on a bureau, or to group candles together on a table. Place a tray on an ottoman to create an additional surface for drinks or snacks.

68 Buy extra sets of inexpensive silverware, plates, and wineglasses to keep on hand for large parties and entertaining.

69 Always pack a small plastic bag or two in your suitcase for laundry, wet bathing suits, or muddy shoes.

70 Stuff rolled-up socks inside boots to help them keep their shape.

Cleaning

71 Rub your nails with half a lemon to freshen them after gardening or cleaning.

72 To remove dog hair and dust quickly from a rug, run a wet sponge over the top of it.

73 Paint stair risers with colored enamel paint so they'll stand up to scuffs. Better yet, stencil on a pattern, which will help hide marks.

74 Vacuum inside your shoes now and then, since dustballs tend to hide there.

75 Use white correction fluid to mask nicks in white woodwork, doors, or cabinets.

Adding Detail

To give new or featureless rooms a sense of history:

76 Change plain hollow-core front doors to older doors or new, solid paneled doors. Old doors can often be found in salvage yards or even trash bins. Old-fashioned screen doors, glass-paned doors, or louvered doors can make a more interesting choice for interior doors.

77 Add a carved mantelpiece to enrich a plain fireplace, or just to add character to an empty wall.

78 Install moldings at chair-rail, picture-rail, or ceiling height (crown molding) to gracefully age a new room. Lightweight foam or plastic moldings can be painted and often hold up better than wood.

79 Change the knobs or hardware on furniture, doors, or fixtures. Vintage or new glass knobs and brass, chrome, or iron hardware are available at hardware stores, home centers, salvage yards, and through renovator's supply stores.

80 Put in beaded-board wainscoting (up to chair-rail height) for

farmhouse charm—painted wainscoting looks great in kitchens, baths, and more casual rooms. If you're not handy with wood, hire a carpenter to help.

Seasonal Transitions

One of the most natural ways to refresh a room is to let it reflect the shift in seasons.

Some quick-change ideas to make the switch to summer:

81 Take up heavy wool rugs and put down cotton rag rugs or straw matting instead, or leave the floors bare.

82 Switch to lighter-weight white or striped slipcovers, or throw a Marseilles spread over the sofa.

83 Put away needlepoint pillows and wool throws in favor of floral chintzes and awning stripes.

84 Hang a mosquito netting canopy over the bed (pure romance!).

85 Dress the bed in white lacy linens; stow away the duvet and use a light matelasse spread.

86 Put dried flowers, a firescreen, or candles in the fireplace.

87 Open up room arrangements to let in light and air, and take in the view.

88 Bring in color with painted flower pots and urns, splashy vintage floral pillows, and zesty table linens.

89 Take down heavy draperies and hang lace curtains or sheer panels.

90 Surround yourself with flowers—cut from the garden or growing in windowboxes, cachepots, and urns.

91 Borrow touches from the garden in furnishings—wicker chairs, a wrought-iron table—and accents: birdhouses, garden signs, bee skeps.

In winter:

92 Draw furniture more closely together, cozied up to the fireplace, if you have one.

93 Layer a Navajo or Oriental rug over sisal carpeting.

94 Add wintery warmth with velvet slipcovers or curtains, paisley, needlepoint, and animal-print pillows, and mohair and chenille throws.

95 Go for deeper, richer colors—aubergine, burgundy, russet.

96 Use Beacon or camp blankets as throws on chairs, beds, or banisters.

97 Warm up the bed with plaid flannel sheets, wool blankets, heirloom quilts, or a downy duvet.

98 Drape tables with a to-the-floor cloth, an extra "topper," or a blanket.

99 Don't neglect reminders of the outdoors, even in winter: Fill large baskets with oversize pinecones and urns with evergreens or berried branches; brighten bowls with pomegranates, pears, or apples.

100 Use candles to create a warming glow.

Can't-Miss Classics

Buy these, save these, use these. They'll always come in handy, always look great:

- white pitchers and bowls
- benches
- fishing baskets or picnic baskets
- shallow baskets for paperwork
- covered boxes
- oversize mugs (great for bathroom as well as kitchen)
- silver candlesticks
- glass hurricane shades
- peg racks
- old books
- Beacon blankets
- Navajo, Oriental, or kilim rugs—old, holey ones can be cut up for pillows or seat covers, or put on top of tables
- small vases—or things like mint julep cups to use for flowers
- trays—wooden, wicker, or silver

Can't-Miss Classic Fabrics

- white cotton duck
- homespun
- matelassé bedspreads
- faded floral chintz
- white damask
- mattress ticking
- awning stripes

Resource Guide

Alabama

Robert Cargo Folk Art Gallery
2314 6th Street
Tuscaloosa, AL 35401
205-758-8884
Sells: Folk art, paintings, sculptures, 20th-century African-American quilts
By appointment only

Arizona

Razzberries
7033 E. Indian School Road
Scottsdale, AZ 85251
602-990-9047
Sells: Antiques, pre-owned furniture, tassels, trims, lamps, and treasures

Arkansas

Hogan's Antique Furniture
14502 Cantrell Road
Little Rock, AR 72212
501-868-9224
Sells: Eclectic furnishings, glassware

James L. Couch Antiques
PO Box 251391
Little Rock, AR 72225
501-374-4793
Sells: Eclectic antiques

Potential Treasures Antiques
700 N. Van Buren Street
Little Rock, AR 72205
501-663-0608
Sells: Traditional 19th- and 20th-century antiques; vintage linen, lamps, mirrors, sterling, crystal, china

California

Aero
207 Ocean Avenue
Laguna Beach, CA 92651
714-376-0535
Sells: 19th-century Mission Revival architectural pieces, American Arts and Crafts

American Roots
105 W. Chapman
Orange, CA 92666
714-639-3424
Sells: American country antiques, toys, quilts, garden accessories, folk art, architectural elements

Company
612 South LaBrea
Los Angeles, CA 90036
213-935-2330
Sells: Slipcovers, antiques, vintage furniture

Durenberger & Friends
31531 Camino Capistrano
San Juan Capistrano, CA 92675
714-240-5181
Sells: Antiques and decorative arts for the home and garden

East Meets West Antiques
658 North Larchmont Blvd.
Hollywood, CA 90004
213-461-1389
Sells: Antiques, accessories, quilts, textiles, country furnishings, Americana

Liz's Antique Hardware
453 South LaBrea
Los Angeles, CA 90036
213-939-4403
Sells: Original hardware circa 1850–1950 for doors, windows, and furniture; curtains, lighting, bath accessories

Michael S. Smith Incorporated
1454 Fifth Street
Santa Monica, CA 90401
310-656-5733
Sells: Reproduction furniture, rugs

Norma Dee Antiques
862 Prospect Street
LaJolla, CA 92039
619-454-5752
Sells: Americana, Flint glass, historical Staffordshire, early Sandwich glass, baskets

Pottery Barn
PO Box 7044
San Francisco, CA 94120-7044
800-922-5507
Sells: Home furnishings

Tancredi & Morgen (A Country Store)
7174 Carmel Valley Road
Valley Hills Center
Carmel, CA 93923
408-625-4477
Sells: Andrea Dern paintings, country furniture, antique pottery, vintage fabric

Upstairs at Diamond
617 South LaBrea Avenue
Los Angeles, CA 90036
213-933-5551
Sells: Needlepoint pillows, Fortuny lamps, linens, towels, gift items, trims, jewelry

Wild Goose Chase & Sweet William
1936 South Coast Highway
Laguna Beach, CA 92651
714-376-9388
Sells: Antique Americana, quilts, beacon blankets, pre-1900 antiques and painted furniture

Colorado

38 Antiques Ltd.
520 East Hyman Avenue
Aspen, CO 81611
303-925-5885
Sells: Antiques, 17th- to 19th-century furniture, garden statues, Venetian and Florentine pieces, reproductions from England and France

Connecticut

Balcony Antique Shops
81 Albany Turnpike
Route 44
Canton, CT 06019
203-693-2996
Sells: Eclectic antique accessories

George Subkoff
260 Post Road East
Westport, CT 06880
203-227-3515
Sells: Eclectic, late 17th- and 18th-, early 19th-century American, English, and Continental antique furniture and decorative art

Delaware

Bellefont Resale Shop
4000 N. Market Street
Wilmington, DE 19802
302-762-1885
Sells: Antique clocks, hall tables, Mission oak furniture, oil lamps

F.H. Herman Antiques
308 Philadelphia Pike
Wilmington, DE 19809
302-764-5333
Sells: Porcelain, furniture, silver, art glass
By appointment only

Twice Nice Antiques
5714 Kennett Pike
Centreville, DE 19807
302-656-8881
Sells: Chippendale, Federal, Queen Anne furnishings and accessories

District of Columbia

Antiques Anonymous
2627 Connecticut Avenue NW
Washington, DC 20008
202-332-5555
Sells: Eclectic antiques, jewelry

Cherishables
1608 20th Street NW
Washington, DC 20009
202-785-4087
Sells: 18th- and 19th-century American furniture, quilts, and accessories

Michael Getz Antiques
2918 M Street NW
Washington, DC 20007
202-338-3811
Sells: Silver, fireplace equipment, lamps, china

Florida

Antiques & Things
515 Fleming Street
Key West, FL 33040
305-292-1333
Sells: Furniture, glassware, jewelry, furniture, prints and paintings

Wisteria Corner Antique Mall
225 North Main
High Springs, FL 32643
904-454-3555
Sells: American and European antiques, collectibles, handcrafted items

Georgia

Atlanta Antiques Exchange
1185 Howell Mill Road NW
Atlanta, GA 30318
404-351-0727
Sells: 19th- and 20th-century English, Oriental, Continental pottery and porcelain

Jacqueline Adams Antiques
2300 Peachtree Road NW
Atlanta, GA 30309
404-355-8123
Sells: Country and French antiques, porcelain, crystal, silver, antique garden accessories

Levison & Cullen Gallery (Deanne Levison)
2300 Peachtree Road
Suite C-101
Atlanta, GA 30309
404-351-3435
Sells: American antique and decorative art from 18th and 19th century, collectibles

Idaho

Michel's Inc.
PO Box 1597
Sun Valley, ID 83353
208-726-8382
Sells: French and English country antiques

Sioux Antiques
8 North Main Street
PO Box 635
Victor, ID 83455
208-787-2644
Sells: Rustic furniture, Western oak and pine furniture, antique kitchen accessories

Illinois

Joanne Boardman Antiques
522 Joanne Lane
Dekalb, IL 60115
815-756-9359
Sells: Country furniture and accessories, New England painted furniture

Mark & Lisa McCormick
8837 Schmaltz
St. Jacob, IL 62281
618-667-7789
Sells: Folk art, painted antique furniture, paintings by Mark McCormick

Frank & Barbara Pollack
1214 Green Bay Road
Highland Park, IL 60035
708-433-2213
Sells: American antiques and art
By appointment only

Indiana

Doug & Jackie Eichhorn
Webb's Antique Mall
200 Union Street
Centerville, IN 47330
317-855-2489
Sells and collects: 20th-century American folk art, late 1940's–1950's American designer furniture and accessories

Heirloom Antiques
3414 N. Shadeland Avenue #C
Indianapolis, IN 46226
317-542-8700
Sells: Antique ink wells, dolls, Victorian accessories, glassware
By appointment only

Indianapolis Downtown Antiques
1044 Virginia Avenue
Indianapolis, IN 46203
317-635-5336
Sells: 1900–1930's furniture, blue/white stoneware, McCoy pottery, oak furniture

Rod Lich & Susan Parrett
2164 Canal Lane
Georgetown, IN 47122
812-738-1858
Sells: Folk art, rustic furniture, American country furniture
By appointment only

Iowa

Bartlett's Quilts
820 35th Street
Des Moines, IA 50312
515-255-1362
Sells: Quilts

Red Ribbon Antiques
812 Washington-Highway 163
Pella, IA 50129
515-628-2181
Sells: Primitive, Victorian antiques, vintage dishes

Snusville Antiques
852 Hull Avenue
Des Moines, IA 50316
515-265-5799
Sells: Eclectic antiques

Kansas

Antique Plaza of Topeka
2935 SW Topeka Boulevard
Topeka, KS 66611
913-267-7411
Sells: American country furniture, fine Victorian furniture, cut glass

Family Affair Antique Mall
3300 West Sixth Avenue SW
Topeka, KS 66604
913-233-8822
Sells: Depression glass, 1920's–1930's furniture, tea sets, matchbox cars, toys

Old World Antiques Ltd.
4436 State Line Road
Kansas City, KS 66103
913-677-4744
Sells: French Old World antiques, furnishings, and accessories

Kentucky

Den of Steven Antiques Mall
945 Baxter Avenue
Louisville, KY 40204
505-458-9581
Sells: Eclectic furnishings (Federal, Victorian, English, French), china, silver, crystal

Jayne Thompson Antiques
847 Kennedy Bridge Road
Harrodsburg, KY 40330
606-748-5628
Sells: Fine antique furniture and accessories

Ruth C. Scully Antiques
5237 Bardstown Road
Louisville, KY 40291
502-491-9601
Sells: Early 19th-century furniture, decorative arts, textiles, Nantucket baskets, folk art
By appointment only

Yesterday Antiques
PO Box 135
Burgin, KY 40310
606-748-5588
Sells: Country and primitive furniture and accessories

Louisiana

Mac Maison, Ltd.
3963 Magazine Street
New Orleans, LA 70115
504-891-2863
Sells: Antiques, lighting, architectural artifacts, and ornamentations

Patout Antiques
929 rue Royal
New Orleans, LA 70116
504-522-0582
Sells: Antiques and accessories from Southern plantations

Wirthmore Antiques
5723 Magazine Street
New Orleans, LA 70015
504-897-9727
Sells: 18th- and 19th-century French Provincial furniture

Maine

Barbara Doherty
PO Box 974
Kennybunkport, ME 04046
207-967-4673
Sells: 18th century country furniture and folk art
By appointment only

Marston House
Main Street
Wiscasset, ME 04578
207-882-6010
Sells: Primarily late 18th- and 19th-century furniture in original paint, accessories, textiles

Riverbank Antiques
Wells Union Antique Center on Rt. 1
Wells, ME 07090
207-646-6314
Sells: English, French, Italian garden architectural elements and decorative antiques

Maryland

All of Us Americans Folk Art
PO Box 30440
Bethesda, MD 20824
301-652-4626
Sells: Southern antique furniture, wood figures, quilts, paintings, weather vanes, American Indian items
By appointment only

Annapolis Antique Shop
20 Riverview Avenue
Annapolis, MD 21401
410-266-5550
Sells: Eclectic furnishings and accessories

Another Period In Time
1708 Fleet Street
Baltimore, MD 21231
410-675-4776
Sells: 1780's and 1950's furniture, including Chippendale and Victorian

Antique Galleria
853 N. Howard Street
Baltimore, MD 21201
410-462-6365
Sells: Eclectic accessories, including English china, art deco, silver plate, pottery

Massachusetts

As Time Goes By
12 Parker Street
Springfield, MA 01151
413-596-4553
Sells: Collectibles, glassware, country, period pieces from the 1930's and 1940's
By appointment only

Boston Antique Center Inc.
54 Canal Street
Boston, MA 02114
614-742-1400
Sells: 18th- to 20th-century quality pieces, paintings, silver, porcelain, mirrors, Oriental rugs

Charles River Antiques
45 River Street
Beacon Hill
Boston, MA 02108
617-367-3244
Sells: Architectural elements, European painted cupboards, landscape elements

Circa Prescott Meiselman, Inc.
PO Box 246
Natick, MA 01760
508-651-3101
Sells: Pre-18th-century antique furniture, accessories, lighting, paintings

Essentials
88 Main Street
No. Hampton, MA 01060
413-584-2327
Sells: Furniture, handmade tables, ceramics, garden accessories

Michigan
Rage of the Age
314 South Ashley Street
Ann Arbor, MI 48104
313-662-0777
Sells: Vintage antique clothing and textiles

Slightly Tarnished-Used Goods
2006 E. Michigan Avenue
Lansing, MI 48912
517-485-3599
Sells: Variety of used goods, including antique lamps and furniture

Minnesota
Antiques Minnesota
1197 University Avenue W
St. Paul, MN 55104
612-646-0037
Sells: Glassware, pottery, ceramics, furniture, jewelry, toys

Past, Present, Future
336 E. Franklin Avenue
Minneapolis, MN 55404
612-870-0702
Sells: Antique, vintage office furniture, Mission oak, antique building materials
By appointment only

Yankee Peddler Antiques
5008 Xerxes Avenue S
Minneapolis, MN 55410
612-926-1732
Sells: Primitive American antiques

Missouri
Antiques & More
2309 Cherokee Street
St. Louis, MO 63118
314-773-1150
Sells: 1950's and 1960's furniture, cut glass, signs, art pottery

Cummings Corner
1703 West 45th Street
Kansas City, MO 64111
816-753-5353
Sells: 1940's Americana, restored light fixtures, quilts

English Garden Antiques
1906 Cherokee Street
St. Louis, MO 63118
314-771-5121
Sells: Old books, china, silver plate, crystal, old prints, lace
By appointment only

Memories & Wishes Antiques
307 Marshall Street
Jefferson City, MO 65101
314-635-8944
Sells: Furniture, glassware, clocks, mirrors, pictures

Montana
Jerome House Antiques
1721 Highland Street
Helena, MT 59601
406-442-1776
Sells: Furniture, documents, fine china, glass, primitives, and clocks
By appointment only

Nebraska
Antique Haven
1723 Vinton Street
Omaha, NE 68108
402-341-8661
Sells: Collectibles
By appointment only

Flea Market Emporium
3235 South 13th Street
Lincoln, NE 68502
402-423-5380
Sells: Basic antiques and collectibles

I Remember Antiques
6571 Maple Street
Omaha, NE 68104
402-556-6061
Sells: Collectibles, including Fiestaware, Red Wing, kitchen items from the 1930's and 1940's

Nevada
Frontier Antique Mall
221 South Curry Street
Carson City, NV 89721
702-887-1466
Sells: Antiques and collectibles of all kinds

Granny's Nook & Cranny
Gypsy Caravan Mall
Las Vegas, NV 89104
702-598-1983
Sells: Victorian, mahogany furniture, jewelry

Old West Antiques
111 Rice Street
Carson City, NV 89706
702-882-4650
Sells: Western antiques, glassware, silver, china, paintings

New Hampshire
Bert Savage Larch Lodge
Route 26
Center Strafford, NH 03815
603-269-7411
Sells: Antique rustic furniture and accessories, antique canoes
By appointment only

New Jersey
Americana by the Seashore
604 Broadway
Barnegat Light, NJ 08006
609-494-0656
Sells: 19th-century oyster plates, antique cupboards, glassware, quilts, pillows, pictures

Greenwood Antiques
1918 Greenwood Avenue
Trenton, NJ 08609
609-586-6887
Sells: American and European paintings
By appointment only

King Charles Ltd.
48 Coryell Street
Lambertville, NJ 08530
609-397-9733
Sells: 18th- and 19th-century English and Continental furniture and accessories

New Mexico
Antique & Almost
1433 San Mateo Boulevard NE
Albuquerque, NM 87110
505-256-3600
Sells: Furniture, jewelry, depression glass, flatware, silverplate, sterling silver
By appointment only

El Paso Import Company
(NOB Hill Business Center)
Albuquerque, NM 87106
505-265-1160
Sells: Colonial and Ranchero Mexican furniture, ceramics, folk art

Gloria List
223 North Guadalupe #231
Santa Fe, NM 87505
505-988-4002
Sells: Southwest religious art and artifacts
By appointment only

Pegasus Antiques & Collectibles
1372 Cerrillos Road
Santa Fe, NM 87505
505-982-3333
Sells: Southwestern antiques

Roma Antiques
3904 Central Avenue SE
Albuquerque, NM 87108
505-266-6453
Sells: Prints, pinups, articles, primitives, Roseville pottery

New York
America Hurrah
766 Madison Avenue
New York, NY 10021
212-635-1930
Sells: Antiques, quilts, American folk art, Native American art

The American Wing
2415 Main Street
Bridgehampton, NY 11932
516-537-3319
Sells: Mirrors, lamps, wicker, rattan, bamboo furniture, small tables, garden items

Amy Perlin Antiques
1020 Lexington Avenue
New York, NY 10021
212-744-4923
Sells: Eclectic collection of 17th- and 18th-century furniture and objects

Barbara Trujillo
Main Street
Bridgehampton, NY 11932
516-537-3838
Sells: Museum-quality antiques, holiday memorabilia, turquoise Indian jewelry, American antiques

Casa El Patio
38 Newtown Lane
Easthampton, NY 11937
516-329-0300
Sells: McCoy pottery, candles, antique painted furniture, accessories

Distant Origin
153 Mercer Street
New York, NY 10012
212-491-0024
Sells: Rustic antiques

English Country Antiques
PO Box 1995
Snake Hollow Road
Bridgehampton, NY 11932
516-537-0606
Sells: Antiques, upholstered
furniture, linen, rugs, wicker
accessories

Hope & Wilder Home
454 Broome Street
New York, NY 10013
212-966-9010
Sells: Antique cupboards,
accessories, vintage and new
fabrics

Laura Fisher
1050 Second Avenue
Gallery #84
New York, NY 10022
212-838-2596
Sells: Antique quilts, Americana,
hooked rugs, folk art

MXYPLYZYK
125 Greenwich Avenue
New York, NY 10014
212-989-4300
Sells: Eclectic bath, tabletop,
lighting items

Paris Images
170 Bleecker Street
New York, NY 10012
212-473-7552
Sells: Contemporary and vintage
custom framing

Ruby Beets Antiques
Poxybogue Road & 27
Bridgehampton, NY 14873
516-537-2802
Sells: Kitchen/bath antiques,
metal furniture, slipcovered easy
chairs, French provincial furniture

Sage Street Antiques
Corner. of Rt. 114 and Sage
Street
Sag Harbor, NY 11963
516-725-4036
Sells: Country antiques, kitchen
kitsch, framed antique prints,
treasures at yard-sale prices

**Susan P. Meisel Decorative
Arts**
133 Prince Street
New York, NY 10012
212-254-0137
Sells: Collectibles, including sail-
boats, Clarice Cliff pottery, original pinup art

Susan Parrish
390 Bleecker Street
New York, NY 10014
212-645-5020
Sells: Antique quilts, folk art,
American Indian art

Treillage Ltd.
418 East 75th Street
New York, NY 10021
212-535-2288
Sells: Garden antiques

Tucker Robbins
366 West 15th Street
New York, NY 10011
212-366-4427
Sells: Southeast, Asian, African,
Latin antiques

**Wolfman Gold & Good
Company**
117 Mercer Street
New York, NY 10012
212-966-7055
Sells: China, linen, upholstered
furniture, flatware, birdhouses/
feeders

Zona
97 Greene Street
New York, NY 10012
212-925-6750
Sells: Southwestern home
accessories, furniture, jewelry

North Carolina
Carolina Collectibles
11717 Six Forks Road
Raleigh, NC 27614
919-848-3778
Sells: 1920's–1930's furniture
By appointment only

Westmoore Pottery
4622 Busbee Road
Seagrove, NC 27341
910-464-3700
Sells: Handmade and hand-
decorated salt-glazed stoneware
in 17th–19th-century styling

North Dakota
Le Fabeargé Antique Mall
200 West Main Avenue
Bismarck, ND 58501
701-221-2594
Sells: Glassware, French enam-
elware, 1850's–1960's furniture

Wizard of Odds 'N Ends
1523 East Thayer Avenue
Bismarck, ND 58501
701-222-4175
Sells: Antique accessories

Ohio
Antiques Etcetera Mall
3265 North High Street
Columbus, OH 43202
614-447-2242
Sells: Primitive furniture, pottery,
Southwestern jewelry

Susie & Rich Burmann
118 South Barron Street
Eaton, OH 45320
513-456-1669
Sells: American 18th- and 19th-
century furniture and accessories
By appointment only

M. Dallas
PO Box 278
Danville, OH 43014
614-599-5919
Sells: Flag plates, antique repro-
duction spatterware

Marjorie Staufer
2244 Remsen Road
Medina, OH 44256
330-239-1443
Sells: American 18th- and 19th-
century furniture and smalls in
original paints and finishes
By appointment only

Robert Zollinhoffer
3845 Fenn Road
Medina, OH 44256
330-722-7544
Sells: Pilgrim century primitives
By appointment only

Oklahoma
Apple Tree Antique Mall
1111 North Meridian Avenue
Oklahoma City, OK 73107
Sells: A variety of collectibles

Tomorrow Memories Antiques
411 Northwest 23rd Street
Oklahoma City, OK 73103
Sells: 1940's furniture, depression glassware, turn of the century collectibles

Oregon
Stars & Splendid Antique Mall
7027 Southeast Milwaukee
Avenue
Portland, OR 97202
503-239-0346
Sells: Extraordinary junk and
collectibles

The Withie's
5655 Suncreek Drive
Lake Oswego, OR 97035
503-620-0404
Sells: Custom silk florals
By appointment only

Pennsylvania
Lewis Keister Antiques
209 Market Street
Lewisburg, PA 17837
717-523-3945
Sells: Textiles, quilts, accessories

Judy Naftulin
7044 Ferry Road
New Hope, PA 18938
215-297-0702
Sells: European and American
furniture, lighting, architectural
elements, garden ornaments,
mirrors, frames, textiles

Period Furniture Designs
102 East Street Road
Kennett Square, PA 19348
610-444-6780
Sells: 18th- and 19th-century
reproduction furniture and
folk art

Rhode Island
Cat's Pajamas
227 Wickenden Street
Providence, RI 02903
401-751-8440
Sells: 20th century antiques
such as silver jewelry, Russel
Wright pottery, glassware, chenille spreads

My Favorite Things
67 Weybossett Street (The
Arcade)
Providence, RI 02903
401-831-3332
Sells: Antique linens, lace, buttons, costume jewelry

South Carolina
Attic Fanatic Antique Malls
935 South Broad Street
Camden, SC 29020
803-787-9856
Sells: Period furniture, art glass,
toys, Belleck porcelain

**Heirloom Antiques &
Collectibles**
6000 Garners Ferry Road
Columbia, SC 29209
803-776-3955
Sells: Bric-a-brac, 1700's furniture, antique jewelry

Thieves Market
502 Gadsden Street
Columbia, SC 29201
803-254-4997
Sells: Furniture, dinnerware,
accessories

South Dakota

Antique & Furniture Mart
1112 West Main Street
Rapid City, SD 57701
605-341-3345
Sells: Turn-of-the-century oak furniture, collectibles, glassware, dishware

Gaslight Antiques
13490 Main Street
Rapid City, SD 57701
605-343-9276
Sells: 1880's–1950's furniture, glassware, jewelry

Tennessee

Antique Merchant's Mall
2015 8th Avenue South
Nashville, TN 37204
615-292-7811
Sells: Rare books, mahogany, walnut and oak furniture, porcelain, china, crystal, sterling

Cane Ery Antique Mall
2207 21st Avenue South
Nashville, TN 37212
615-269-4780
Sells: American primitive and oak furniture, cane and basket repair and supplies

Hunter Kay Woodland Antiques
5180 Firetower Road
Franklin, TN 37064
615-794-6450
Sells: Eclectic antiques

Joy Haley
102 Brighton Close
Nashville, TN 37205
615-297-6364
Sells: High end country painted furniture and accessories

Texas

Antique Center of Texas
1001 West Loop North
Houston, TX 77055
713-688-4211
Sells: Eclectic antiques

James Powell
715 West Avenue
Austin, TX 78701
512-477-9939
Sells: 17th- and 18th-century continental furniture and accessories

John Holt Antiques
2416 Woodhead
Houston, TX 77019
713-528-5065
Sells: Religious art, primitives

Pier 1 Imports
PO Box 962030
Fort Worth, TX 76161-0020
800-447-4371
Sells: Home furnishings and accessories

Room Service by Ann Fox
4354 Lover's Lane
Dallas, TX 75225
214-369-7666
Sells: Antique beds, great new fabrics, paintings, vintage memorabilia

Shabby Slips
2304 Bissonnet
Houston, TX 77005
713-630-0066
Sells: Aged painted furniture, custom slipcovers, architectural elements, mirrors

True West
Rt. 3, Box 177-A
Goldwaite, TX 76844
915-648-2696
Sells: Western, Santa Fe, American country antiques

Uncommon Market
2701 Fairmount
Dallas, TX 75201
214-871-2775
Sells: Decorative antiques

Waterbird Traders
3420 Greenville Avenue
Dallas, TX 75206
214-821-4606
Sells: Fine American Indian, Spanish Colonial, primitive art, and antiques

Utah

Pine Cupboard Antiques
247 East 300 South
Salt Lake City, UT 84111
801-359-6420
Sells: Pine furniture and Utah art

Salt Lake Antiques
279 East 300 South
Salt Lake City, UT 84111
801-322-1273
Sells: Early English and American antiques, Persian rugs, silver, paintings

Vermont

Glad Rags Fine Vintage Antiques
6 State Street
Montpelier, VT 05602
802-223-1451
Sells: Lamps, art pottery, postcards, jewelry, glass, china, metal through deco period

Sylvan Hill Antiques
Sylvan Road
Grafton, VT 05146
802-875-3954
Sells: Period English and American country furniture specializing in children's furniture
By appointment only

The Clock Doctor Inc.
South Street
Middletown Springs, VT 05143
802-235-2440
Sells: Antique mechanical clocks

Virginia

Baron's Antiques and Collectibles
1706 East Main Street
Richmond, VA 23223
804-643-0001
Sells: Eclectic

Franklin Antiques
Route 1, Box 1870
Rocky Mount, VA 24151
703-334-5448
Sells: 18th- and 19th-century southern American antiques and accessories

Lane Sanson
3423 West Cary Street
Richmond, VA 23221
804-358-0053
Sells: Eclectic antique accessories as well as outdoor hand-painted furniture

West End Antiques
6504 Horsepen Road
Richmond, VA 23229
804-285-1916
Sells: Eclectic antiques, country primitive, glassware, oak and wicker furnishings

Washington

Fircrest Country Store
612 Regents Boulevard
Fircrest, WA 98466
206-566-6886
Sells: Antiques, collectibles, gifts

Island Lady Antiques
55 Second Street
PO Box 3233
Friday Harbor, WA 98250
206-378-2890
Sells: American country antiques

Ruby Montana's Pinto Pony, Ltd.
603 Second Avenue
Seattle, WA 98104
206-621-PONY
Sells: 1950's accessories, 1930's–1960's furniture, Western nostalgia

West Virginia

Smokey J Antics
600 Sissonville Drive
Sissonville, WV 25312
304-984-9783
Sells: Dolls, old toys, trunks, rocking chairs, clocks

Split Rail Antiques
2580 Benson Drive
Charleston, WV 25302
304-342-6084
Sells: Country antiques, early sporting items
By appointment only

Wisconsin

Antiques Mall of Madison
4748 Cottage Grove Road
Madison, WI 53716
608-222-2049
Sells: Eclectic

Larry's Used Furniture
2898 South Syene Road
Madison, WI 53711
608-271-8162
Sells: Doors, windows, furniture, rugs

Past Recollections
5735 South 27th Street
Greenfield, WI 53221
414-281-3099
Sells: Primitive pieces,dishware, lamps, rugs

Wyoming

Old West Antiques & Cowboy Collectibles
1215 Sheridan Avenue
Cody, WY 82414
307-587-9014
Sells: Western antiques and collectibles

Tomorrow's Treasures Antiques
903 East Lincolnway
Cheyenne, WI 82001
307-634-1900
Sells: General line of antiques, glassware, and pottery

Index